REVERSE WINE SNOB

How to Buy and Drink Great Wine Without Breaking the Bank

JON THORSEN

Skyhorse Publishing

Skyhorse Publishing books may be purchased in bulk at special discounts for sales promotion, corporate gifts, fund-raising, or educational purposes. Special editions can also be created to specifications. For details, contact the Special Sales Department, Skyhorse Publishing, 307 West 36th Street, 11th Floor, New York, NY 10018 or info@skyhorsepublishing.com.

Skyhorse® and Skyhorse Publishing® are registered trademarks of Skyhorse Publishing, Inc.®, a Delaware corporation.

Visit our website at www.skyhorsepublishing.com.

10 9 8 7 6 5 4 3 2 1

Library of Congress Cataloging-in-Publication Data is available on file.

Cover design by Mary Belibasakis

ISBN: 978-1-63220-681-7
Ebook ISBN: 978-1-63220-923-8

Printed in China

CONTENTS

INTRODUCTION

URBANDICTIONARY.COM DEFINES A WINE SNOB as "a wine enthusiast, particularly one who is pretentious, or self-important because of their 'immense wine knowledge.'"

We all know the type. Perhaps it's your uncle or a friend who once vacationed in Bordeaux and has now become the overbearing know-it-all who can't open a bottle without first giving a lecture. The bane of average wine consumers everywhere, wine snobs love to point out just how superior their $75 bottle of wine is to your $10 one.

Still, I have to admit there is a bit of good in wine snobbery—the enthusiasm. There's certainly nothing wrong with being enthusiastic about wine, right? It's the pretentious and self-important parts of wine snobbery that most of us can't stand—the belittling of someone's chosen drink and the supremely false belief that expensive is always better.

My solution to this problem is to simply turn wine snobbery upside down—to become a "Reverse Wine Snob." I am a wine enthusiast for sure, but a wine enthusiast with an open mind and a reasonable budget!

I am simply a wine consumer. I have no special training or tasting powers. I don't have any certifications or fancy letters after my name; in fact, I've never even taken a "wine appreciation" class. I'm not able to tell you the region or variety of a wine just by sniffing it. I'm just a guy who loves to drink wine and tell people about the good, cheap ones. I love saving money and not overpaying for things.

Several years ago, after constantly hearing about all the health benefits of wine, and knowing that heart disease ran in my wife Brenda's family, we decided that we should drink wine more often. After we realized that three or four $20 bottles a week was going to quickly blow apart our budget, I went on a search for great, inexpensive wine that we could use as a "daily drinker". Like most people we assumed you had to spend $15–$20 on a bottle to get a quality wine. After all, the cheapest bottles on restaurant wine lists were often more than this. (We'll talk about why that is later.) We didn't expect to find much and thought our adventure with wine was going to be a short one, but we were pleasantly surprised to find that there is a ton of really good, inexpensive wine out there. Once we made that discovery we knew we had to tell others, and my website ReverseWineSnob.com was born.

Thanks to the success of my website I have wine sent to me from all over the world. I've also had the opportunity to travel to well-known wine regions like California and France as well as lesser-known wine regions like Virginia and Slovenia. This has given me the opportunity to try almost two hundred different grape varieties in just the last few years, from every possible price range! I've tasted tons of wine now, much of it bad but some of it good.

My objective in writing this book is simple—to get more people to enjoy the world of wine. I figure if people are like me (a truly frightening thought indeed!) there are a good number of you who would drink more wine if you just knew that you didn't have to spend a small fortune to enjoy a glass of wine with dinner every night.

This is not a book that sets out to explain every wine term or to give a comprehensive review of all wine regions. This is a book designed to set you free from the notion that you have to be an expert to drink wine and that you have to spend big bucks for a good bottle. I am a staunch believer in learning through drinking (what could be more fun!), so much of the information shared in this book is through my wine reviews. I encourage you to try out some of these recommended bottles and learn right alongside us.

The book starts with my unique rating system that builds price into the equation—the more expensive the bottle, the better it has to be to garner a "recommended buy" rating! This would seem like common sense, but it's bordering on radical in the world of wine. The book then hones in on my "Ten Tenets of Reverse Wine Snobbery," beliefs I hold dear that likely fly in the face of much of what you will read in other wine books.

From there we'll take a quick look at some basic wine terms and then dive into region by region highlights of the very best wines under $20. Since getting the best deal on a bottle is critical to our mission, we'll then turn to buying wine. We'll examine where to find the wine we recommend and how to buy wine online, and take a deeper dive into wines exclusive to two of the biggest retailers out there—Costco and Trader Joe's. (Plus some hints on how to use their unique pricing models to your advantage.) We'll then wrap up our exploration with a look at the wine snobs number one target of derision: box wine.

Still wondering if this is the right book for you? This book is not directed at the established wine aficionado. This is a book for the average Joe who just wants to know that the $10 or so he plunks down for a bottle of wine is going to be well spent. And on the rare occasion that he spends $20 on a bottle, it's going to be much better than the $10 one. Far too often it's not and we're here to help fix that.

Cheers!
Jon

CHAPTER 1

THE RATING SYSTEM

AT ITS HEART, OUR RATING system is fairly simple and admittedly a bit subjective. It's simple by design. With a background in analytics, my first inclination is to design an extremely complex formula, analogous to, say, the convoluted QB rating in football that no one can understand. Instead I decided it's best to keep a wine rating system as basic as possible. All wines are rated on two factors: taste and cost. From there I came up with an algorithm that combines both of these into one overall rating.

THE TASTE RATING

A simple scale from 1–10. I'm endlessly confused by the 100-point rating system given by the major wine magazines and critics. If you have 100 points, why are 80 percent of wines rated between 85 and 94? Simplify, simplify, simplify. This rating is subjective, so your opinion may vary.

THE COST (VALUE) RATING

Again, a 1–10 scale, but as price goes up, the rating goes down.

Bottle Price	Value Rating
<$6.00	10
$6.00 - $7.99	9
$8.00 - $9.99	8
$10.00 - $11.99	7
$12.00 - $13.99	6
$14.00 - $15.99	5
$16.00 - $16.99	4
$17.00 - $17.99	3
$18.00 - $18.99	2
$19.00 - $19.99	1

THE OVERALL RATING

To score really high, a wine must be cheap and good. The more expensive the wine gets, the harder it is to attain a high score (unless the taste rating is off the charts, which is the way it should be, right?). We're trying to maximize our dollars here!

The Reverse Wine Snob Rating System

		Taste Rating ———>									
Bottle Price	Cost Rating	10	9	8	7	6	5	4	3	2	1
$6.00	10	10.0	9.3	8.5	7.8	7.0	6.3	5.5	4.8	4.0	3.3
$6.00-$7.99	9	9.8	9.0	8.3	7.5	6.8	6.0	5.3	4.5	3.8	3.0
$8.00-$9.99	8	9.5	8.8	8.0	7.3	6.5	5.8	5.0	4.3	3.5	2.8
$10.00-$11.99	7	9.3	8.5	7.8	7.0	6.3	5.5	4.8	4.0	3.3	2.5
$12.00-$13.99	6	9.0	8.3	7.5	6.8	6.0	5.3	4.5	3.8	3.0	2.3
$14.00-$15.99	5	8.8	8.0	7.3	6.5	5.8	5.0	4.3	3.5	2.8	2.0
$16.00-$16.99	4	8.5	7.8	7.0	6.3	5.5	4.8	4.0	3.3	2.5	1.8
$17.00-$17.99	3	8.3	7.5	6.8	6.0	5.3	4.5	3.8	3.0	2.3	1.5
$18.00-$18.99	2	8.0	7.3	6.5	5.8	5.0	4.3	3.5	2.8	2.0	1.3
$19.00-$19.99	1	7.8	7.0	6.3	5.5	4.8	4.0	3.3	2.5	1.8	1.0
$20.00+	0	7.5	6.8	6.0	5.3	4.5	3.8	3.0	2.3	1.5	0.8

8.3 - 10	Bulk Buy!
7.8 - 8.2	Highly Recommended
7.0 - 7.7	Recommended Buy
6.0 - 6.9	Second Chance?
6.0	Skip It

THE RECOMMENDATIONS

8.3–10: Bulk Buy! (Buy as much as you can because it's awesome)

7.8–8.2: Highly Recommended (Grab a few)

7.0–7.7: Recommended Buy (Buy a bottle)

6.0–6.9: Give it a second chance?

6.0: Skip it

CHAPTER 2

TEN TENETS OF REVERSE WINE SNOBBERY

T HERE'S NO BETTER PLACE TO begin our journey than with my *Ten Tenets of Reverse Wine Snobbery*. These are ten beliefs that I hold dear—that likely fly in the face of much of what you read in the big wine magazines and websites. The reason people buy and drink wine is to enjoy it. Sure, there are some people that buy big-name bottles as a status symbol or even an investment, but for most of us we're spending our hard earned money to consume something from which we derive pleasure. Unfortunately, the wine industry gets in its own way by intimidating and looking down on the average consumer. Opening most wine magazines is an exercise in discouragement as you're flooded with articles about ultra-expensive and high-scoring wines that are hopelessly out of your price range. My hope and goal is that by the time you're done reading through these Ten Tenets you'll be truly free to enjoy wine on your own terms!

TENET #1: BUY WINE THAT FITS YOUR LIFESTYLE; DON'T CHANGE YOUR LIFESTYLE TO FIT YOUR WINE.

For most of us, a "good" wine is one that you can enjoy on any or no occasion, pair with normal food (or no food at all!), drink from basic, inexpensive (even [*gasp*] dishwasher-safe!) wineglasses, and feel good about it.

A couple years ago, I was invited to a large wine tasting with the head of a major wineglass company. The point of the tasting was to show how several varieties of wine taste better in specifically designed glasses. The way this man worked the room with the power of suggestion was simply masterful. It was almost like watching a hypnotist at work as he described exactly what we would (or "should") taste as we tried each wine in a normal glass and then in the "perfect" stemware. I was amazed not by the difference in taste in each glass (which was marginal at best) but by the people's heads bobbing in agreement before they even tasted the wine!

Essentially, though there were differences in each glass, they were very minor—and this was with a $200 bottle of wine, in an isolated environment, solely focused on the wine itself to decipher even the slightest differences—definitely not the way most people drink their wine!

Our number one rule for stemware is that it be dishwasher safe. For us that means stemless glasses from Costco. In fact, I've got a whole shelf full of fancy wineglasses designed for every varietal imaginable that I've gotten as freebies and I never use them. What parent of three children wants to spend his or her alone time every night hand-washing wineglasses? Not me.

Another example is pairing food and wine. The best food and wine pairing is always the one YOU like the best. Furthermore, don't fall into the trap of thinking that you need to pair your wine with food at all. The French would be disgusted to hear it, but if you're like most, you do the majority of your wine drinking without food, and that is perfectly fine. That's not to say that that the right combination of wine and food is not a wonderful thing, because it certainly is and we'll let you know some of our favorites throughout the book. Everyone's preferences vary, so don't feel locked in to a specific pairing just because they are supposed to go together. Do what feels right to you.

A food and wine pairing is about the pairing, not the individual components. A great example is wine and chocolate. Every

Valentine's Day we get the requisite stories on wine and chocolate pairings, but on the other 364 days of the year a recent trend is to heartily expound on why wine and chocolate don't work together. Port and chocolate sure, the wine snobs say, but wine and chocolate—never! "It will ruin the wine!" As much as I love wine, which is a lot, the primary component for me in this pairing is the chocolate. I love chocolate. And if a wine can add another layer of complexity or taste to the chocolate, well then that's awesome. Who cares if the wine itself is not primary; it's the combination I'm after.

Some wine and chocolate favorites for me include Syrah with spicy dark chocolate—the little spicy kick goes wonderfully with a smoky, peppery Syrah. Pinot Noir with white chocolate is delicious. (Yes, white chocolate is actually good for something!) And try Petite Sirah with any type of chocolate. Just ask my oldest daughter how much I like this pairing and she'll tell you about the time her Easter bunnies were the only chocolate to be found in the house . . .

And no, I didn't really eat the head off my daughter's chocolate bunny— what kind of dad would do that? Now if it had been dark chocolate that might be another story. . . .

TENET #2: DRINK WHAT YOU LIKE.

Since we're open-minded wine drinkers, our number one rule of wine tasting is drink whatever the heck you like. If you don't like red wines, no problem. If you don't like dry wines, don't drink them. Why would anyone in his or her right mind drink or eat something intended to be pleasurable if they don't like it? We're not talking about vegetables here! If syrupy, sugary sweet Moscato with an ice cube is your thing, go to town. Likewise if it is vintage Châteauneuf-du-Pape.

Many wine drinkers undermine their own tastes by listening to experts. Not to undercut anyone's credibility, but the fact is those so-called "experts" are simply not very reliable. Recently retired statistics professor turned winery owner Robert Hodgson did a revealing study on the judges at the California State Fair.[1] Since wine judges at the CA State Fair don't know which wine is which when they are tasting them, Mr. Hodgson convinced the wine competition organizers to let him re-insert the same wine back into the tasting lineups to see if the judges' scores would be consistent. The result was wildly different scores for the same wine when tasted on different occasions.

Mr. Hodgson then turned his attention to wine competitions in general and found that the awarding of gold medals was statistically a random process! Virtually all wines that receive a gold medal at one competition received no medals at other competitions: "One winery entered 14 competitions and got no awards in 13 of them, and got a gold medal in the 14th. Guess what's on the label of that wine? Gold medal winner."

This brings up a very important point. Many people would be surprised to know that at most of these wine competitions and in many wine reviews for the big magazines, dozens and dozens of wines are tasted at a time. Often each wine is only given a few sips.

---

1 Controversial Wine Judging Study: The Real Story by W. Blake Gray at Wine-Searcher.com. http://www.wine-searcher.com/m/2013/07/controversial-wine-judging-study-the-real-story

(And we're using the word "sip" loosely here because usually the wine is sniffed and then swirled around in the reviewer's mouth before being spit out.) It's no wonder then that these judges' scores are inconsistent! I'm sure a wine does taste different when it is the first wine tasted versus when it is the twenty-fifth. This is also the reason why all of my reviews are done based on tasting wine normally—like an average person would. The wine is tasted over a period of a couple hours, often with and without food and then rechecked the next day to see how it held up. After all, if you're like my wife and me, it takes two days to go through a whole bottle of wine. That means it is very helpful to know if that wine you are buying is going to taste just as good on day two as it did when it was first opened. If not, then you've just wasted half your money.

Richard Quandt, the editor of the *Journal of Wine Economics*, said, "Nobody can even identify, with certainty, all the ingredients, all the molecules, in a glass of wine (or beer or gin or whatever). Nobody understands, exactly, why booze tastes the way it does, and why people like it. And nobody understands, exactly, how human beings actually taste things."[2]

Scores and points mean nothing if your tastes are different than whoever is giving those scores and points. Wine is not an objective thing—we all taste and smell differently. We have different preferences based on a myriad of different reasons. For example, I can't stand cigarette smoke; it drives me crazy. Yet, I love the smell of a good cigar because my grandpa smoked cigars and as a little kid I used to love hanging out in the garage talking to him as he smoked.

Wine reviews are great if you can find someone who has similar tastes. If not, they're just irrelevant. I recently came across a review from a major wine magazine that described a wine as having "a note of just-run horse and saddle." Seriously? It smells like

---

2 Wine needs its Nate Silver: Can we quantify and more accurately describe how alcohol tastes? by Adam Rogers in Salon.com. http://www.salon.com/2014/06/22/wine_needs_its_nate_silver_can_we_quantify_and_more_accurately_describe_how_alcohol_tastes/)

sweaty horse? And the average person is supposed to know what horse sweat smells like? Funny thing is they actually liked the wine!

TENET #3: EXPERIMENT WITH NEW WINE.

My wife and I love tasting new wine. How do you know what you like if you don't try lots of things? It's important to push your boundaries; you never know what you might find. Keep an open mind.

Some of my favorite finds have come from the most unexpected varieties and from the most unexpected places. The basics like Cabernet Sauvignon and Chardonnay are not the only drinkable varieties out there. In fact, in many cases these popular varieties are being forced to grow in places ill-suited for them, precisely because wineries think this is what people want. It's supply and demand. And unfortunately, in many cases, wonderful old vine indigenous grapes are torn up and replaced by the popular varieties because that is what sells, even though it makes vastly inferior wine.

Variety and diversity are good. The varieties that will grow and generally taste the best are the ones that are native to that area. There's a reason why each variety developed and remain in a certain place. So don't be afraid of wines made from varieties you've never heard of!

Take for example the Quinta De La Rosa Douro Red from Portugal. It's a blend of three grapes that are likely only familiar to Port drinkers: Touriga Nacional, Touriga Franca, and Tinta Roriz. All three grapes are native to Portugal and are typically planted together in the vineyard in proportions that have been honed over the decades to produce wonderful wines and Ports. Big, rich, and silky, this is one of the first wines that opened my eyes to the amazing value coming out of Portugal. In fact, I liked it so much I gave it a rare 10 rating on my Taste scale. Unfortunately, when most consumers are faced with the decision between something unknown and a tried and true variety like Cabernet Sauvignon, most people fall back on the tried and true. Of course the silver lining in this for Reverse Wine Snobs is that prices stay low on some of these lesser-known gems.

Another example is Spanish Garnacha. The Altovinum Evodia Old Vines Garnacha was one of our very first eye-openers. This wine routinely sells for $8 or less, which is amazing considering that it comes from vines that are up to 100 years old. If you've spent any time in the wine section at your liquor store you've probably seen wine labels loudly proclaiming "Old Vine," "Old Vine"! There's actually a great reason for this—the older a vine gets the deeper and more complex its root system becomes, which allows it to thrive even in adverse conditions. This leads to more consistent grape production each year. In addition, as vines age they tend to produce less fruit, but the grapes that remain have a higher concentration of flavor—perfect for making flavorful wine.

One hundred years old is really old for a vine and in many parts of the world wines made from vines this old command a huge premium. However, this is not always the case in Spain, which has more land planted to vineyards than any other country. Old vine Garnacha is actually pretty routine and abundant in a lot of areas. Those old vines impart deep, rich flavors to the wine that can't be replicated any other way, and vintage after vintage the Evodia continuously delivers tons of savory fruit and spice. (Unfortunately there's no standard agreement on how old is old, so you may want to do a little fact checking into those "old vine" claims you see on the label.)

In addition, regions love to tout marquee varieties (think Cabernet Sauvignon from Napa Valley, Pinot Noir from Oregon, Sauvignon Blanc from New Zealand, or Malbec from Argentina). These are all great and I don't blame regions for promoting these varieties as their specialties, but let's be real. If one variety grows well enough to be a marquee grape, there must be other varieties that grow well there too. Explore the other varieties that regions have to offer beyond just the marquee varieties! A side benefit of this is that you can often save money. Lower demand for lesser-known grape varieties often translates into lower prices.

An example of a wine that completely changed my perception of a region was the Craggy Range Te Kahu Gimblett Gravels Vineyard Proprietary Red from New Zealand. New Zealand is known for its excellent Sauvignon Blanc and really nice, inexpensive Pinot Noir. But not many wine enthusiasts know that New Zealand can also produce a great Bordeaux-style blend of Merlot, Cabernet Franc, Cabernet Sauvignon, and Malbec like this one. This wine blew me away with its enticing aromas of plum, blackberry, spice, and a little vanilla. The wine tastes smooth and rich with luscious fruit flavors and an almost dusty texture that really enhances its complexity while still maintaining its easy-to-drink nature.

Another example is Malbec from Argentina. We love the great selection of Malbec wines from Argentina that are on the market. But Malbec is a grape that originally came from France and is still grown there. There are a number of excellent, nearly forgotten Malbecs from all over France, but the Cahors area is definitely the spot to check out. And speaking of Argentina, as much as we love Malbec, there are other wines made there too! The delicate and very aromatic white variety of Torrontés is a great wine to explore. And on the red side, Bonarda is a widely planted and very under-appreciated grape that sells for next to nothing in this country.

Closer to home, everyone knows California for its Cabernet but our very favorite variety from this diverse region is Petite Sirah. It's the variety that is routinely added to other wines (especially Zinfandel) to give them more structure and boldness, but it's also fabulous on its own. There are tons of really excellent California producers of this wine out there from Pedroncelli in Dry Creek Valley to Concannon in the Livermore Valley to The Crusher in Clarksburg to Michael David Winery in Lodi to Vigilance and Line 39 in Lake County. I encourage you to seek them out and give them a try.

TENET #4: WINE UNDER $20 IS NOT A COMPROMISE. (PRICE DOES NOT EQUAL QUALITY.)

Far too often inexpensive wine is marketed as a shadow of something more expensive. What you may notice if you look closely, however, is that this is usually done by the companies that also sell more expensive wines. There's a simple reason the less expensive bottles are marketed this way—they still want to sell their pricier bottles. If they came right out and said their $12 bottle was every bit as good as their $45 bottle, why would anyone (in his or her right mind) buy the $45 one?

Study after study has shown that when blind tasting a mix of expensive and inexpensive wines virtually no one is any good at picking out the expensive one. Actually, when asked their preference most people will choose the inexpensive one!

One of the most famous examples is discussed in Stephen Dubner and Steven Levitt's book *Freakonomics*.[3] As a member of the Harvard Society of Fellows for several years, Mr. Levitt was not a big fan of the group's custom of contributing his hard-earned money to $60 bottles of wines at its meetings. Since he was unable to talk his way out of the arrangement he developed an alternative strategy where he hosted a blind tasting that, unbeknownst to the tasters, included an incredibly cheap bottle of wine along with two expensive ones. He also split one of the two expensive bottles into two separate decanters to give the illusion that there were actually four different wines.

You can probably guess where this is going . . .

> The results could not have been better for me. There was no significant difference in the rating across the four wines; the cheap wine did just as well as the expensive ones. Even more remarkable, for a given drinker, there was more variation in the rankings they gave to the two samples drawn from the same bottle than there was between any other two samples. Not only did they like

3 http://freakonomics.com/2008/07/16/cheap-wine/

the cheap wine as much as the expensive one, they were not even internally consistent in their assessments.

So not only did the cheap wine rate just as high as the expensive one but tasters didn't even give the same wine the same score when tasting it twice.

There's also the infamous French experiment where testers dyed a white wine red (using a tasteless and odorless dye) and asked wine students (who did not know it was the same wine) to describe it before and after.[4] The result was that students described the very same wine vastly differently solely based on whether they thought they were drinking a white or red wine.

Richard Wiseman, a psychologist at Hertfordshire University in England, tested hundreds of drinkers to determine if they could tell the difference between a cheap wine and a wine that costs two to three times the price.[5] He found that the subjects picked out the more expensive wine only 53 percent of the time—essentially the same rate as if they had simply guessed. He concluded: "Normally when a product is that much more expensive, you would expect to be able to tell the difference." BINGO!

And how about the case where a group of researchers set out to determine if simply knowing the price of a wine before tasting it would change people's perception of it?[6] Using an MRI machine to scan people's brains as they unknowingly tried the same wine at different price points showed that simply telling them that a wine is more expensive actually made their brains think it tastes better!

As an aside you've probably seen this play out yourself every time you go out to a restaurant thanks to the ridiculous markup

---

4 "The Color of Odors" by Gil Morrot, Frédéric Brochet, and Denis Dubourdieu from http://www.daysyn.com/Morrot.pdf

5 "Expensive wine and cheap plonk taste the same to most people" 4/13/2011 from http://www.theguardian.com/science/2011/apr/14/expensive-wine-cheap-plonk-taste

6 "Marketing actions can modulate neural representations of experienced pleasantness" by Hilke Plassmann, John O'Doherty, Baba Shiv, and Antonio Rangel from http://www.pnas.org/content/105/3/1050.

on wine. In fact, if you buy wine at a restaurant you're basically subsidizing all the people only buying food. This is simply because the extremely high margin on alcohol is used to keep margins on food razor thin. That per-glass cost you see on the menu? That is typically the restaurant's cost for the entire bottle! The reasoning behind this: if they open a bottle and pour only one glass out of it that night, they won't lose any money. (What other industry gets away with that kind of pricing strategy?) Ironically, it's the people who do most of their wine drinking in restaurants, buying $40, $50, and $60 bottles, who then turn around and disparage any wine under $20. It turns out the joke is on them because all those bottles they've been wasting their money on retail for $20 or less.

The point of all these stories is simple: If you can simply break yourself of the false belief that the more expensive a wine is the better it will taste, just think how much more enjoyment you would get out of your inexpensive wine *and* how much money you would save!

TENET #5: THE WINE INDUSTRY OFTEN SEEMS TO FORGET ABOUT THE AVERAGE CONSUMER. (HOW TO AVOID THEIR MARKETING TRAPS)

The wine industry has gotten completely caught up in its imagined or ideal wine consumer: the affluent wine geek. In reality, the affluent wine geek is a tiny, minuscule portion of the entire market. This tenet is directed at the wine industry itself, but I include it here because I also think it's educational for the average consumer to know just how the wine industry markets to its audience—and how not to get caught in their traps.

The average bottle of wine sold in the United States costs $6.25. That means the vast majority, estimated at 80–90 percent, of wine sold in the United States is well under $10. Yet wines are generally marketed to look like they cost much more. Admittedly, the tiny slice of the market that buys expensive wine spends an awful lot of money doing it, so I don't blame wineries for targeting this exclusive group. However, I do find it ridiculous that wineries feel the need to copy the marketing plan of a $100 bottle for their $10 to $15 bottles.

Let's take wine labels as an example. First there's the front of the label where terms like *gold edition* or *ultra* are tacked on but have no practical meaning. In many regions terms like *reserva* and *gran reserva* are strictly legislated, and very precise standards must be met in order for wines to be labeled that way. In other regions (like California), it's more like *hey just slap a name on there*! I imagine the marketing meeting going something like this:

> **Marketing Guy #1:** What should we call this $8 bottle of wine?
>
> **Marketing Guy #2:** It's got to be something that makes it seem exclusive . . .
>
> **Marketing Guy #1:** Yeah, but it's only $8 and we made 100,000 cases.
>
> **Marketing Guy #2:** How about we call it a reserva like those Spanish wines!
>
> **Marketing Guy #1:** But those wines need to be aged in oak and bottled for years before being released; our wine is from last year's harvest. And besides, we only have one wine; how can we call it a reserva if it's our only wine?
>
> **Marketing Guy #2:** That decides it then, we'll call it a reserva. Have the labels printed!

Next there's the bottle itself. Have you ever noticed that when placing several wine bottles next to each other even bottles of the same shape can have vastly different sizes and weights? The weight is what really gets to me though. There must be a marketing study somewhere that says consumers equate heavier bottles with higher quality wines because some wineries take this to the extreme. Meanwhile, in my mind I'm thinking about how much of the money I paid for this wine must go to the shipping cost for this extra heavy bottle.

Another marketing trap is the wines are so full of stickers touting those meaningless gold medals and 90+ point ratings that you can barely read the label. But perhaps the worst offender is the back of the bottle. Food pairings are a prime example. I'm sure "prosciutto-wrapped grilled peaches" are delicious, but it's not standard fare at most people's houses. I have no doubt that more people would be buying wine if the wines themselves spoke to their real world situation. What's a good wine for chicken nuggets? Basic spaghetti? Mac and cheese? Burgers and brats? All those meals can be paired wonderfully with wine; I just wish wineries would be willing to tell consumers about it.

TENET #6: THE THREE-TIER SYSTEM SUCKS AND NEEDS TO GO AWAY.

The three-tier system is the distribution system that was put into place in this country following Prohibition. Almost all states follow this system, which essentially separates the "three tiers": producers (wineries and importers), wholesalers/distributors, and retailers. For the most part, each tier's functions are not allowed to cross over into the other. This sounds OK on the surface, but it should also be no surprise that when you legislate, for example, that retailers must buy all their wine from a wholesaler, you give a tremendous amount of power to someone who has no real incentive to work in anyone's interest but his or her own. The interests of consumers (low prices and lots of choices) are nowhere to be found.

Did you know there are over 125,000 different wines produced each year? Yet your average wine store only has a few thousand of them and over half of the wines on their shelves come from only three companies. Much of this has to do with the distribution system in the United States, where there are only around four hundred distributors controlling consumers' access to wine. If your local distributors don't have it (or simply don't want to go through the bother of carrying it in the case of many small brands), you're out of luck unless you live in a state that allows the direct shipment of wine through the mail.

This unnecessary legal protectionism results in situations like what recently happened in Florida, where craft brewers decided it would be nice to sell their own beer from their own tasting rooms. Distributors in Florida balked at this—it would not be safe for the community! The Florida Senate therefore passed bill SB 1714, which called for distributors to operate in a strict order: pick up cases of beer from the brewery, take it to their warehouses, and then deliver the very same cases of beer back to the very same brewery. The bill also mandated that this new structure would result in an astounding 30 percent markup for the distributor for doing nothing but unnecessarily moving around cases of beer!

Although the distributors in Florida suggested the bill was passed to protect the community, that's not true. As Tom Wark suggested on his blog Fermentation, distributors have been protected for so long that they are not even afraid to admit the real reason for the bill: competition! Mitch Rubin, the executive director of the Florida Beer Wholesalers Association. stated the following on WSRQ Sarasota Talk Radio:

> What we're very concerned about is, really what folks do is get a brewery license, get this retail license, but then brew the beer at some centralized facility . . . and then ship the beer into this so-called brewery. Then it goes out to the consumer through the retail portion of the premises in competition with distributors and retailers.[7]

What other industry is entitled to protection like this from competition at the expense of consumers? When I asked winemaker Randall Grahm of Bonny Doon Vineyards about his thoughts on the three-tier system, he stated:

> I'm sure I'm not the first person to come up with this pithy analogy, but the 3-tier system in the U.S. is very much like the

---

7 http://fermentationwineblog.com/2014/04/pulllng-back-curtain-booze-wholesalers-fear-competition/

Mafia—set up to insure that the relevant players, in this instance, the wholesalers who originally designed the system, are insured an orderly allocation of profits (and the assurance that they will ultimately get paid).

I was able to see all of this play out just recently in my neck of the woods as a giant wine retailer opened its first stores and a state-wide beverage association tried to prevent cities from granting them liquor licenses. Why? They fear competition, plain and simple. The beverage association's website proudly proclaims its commitment to protecting its members from competition through legislative lobbying as well as such noble accomplishments as:

1. Fought back attempts to weaken the "three-tiered" alcohol system.
2. Defeated wine in grocery since 2000!
3. Opposed lower blood alcohol levels for DWI and smoking prohibitions.

God forbid wine be sold in grocery stores and that the DWI blood alcohol level be lowered to save more lives! What other retail industry has the luxury of this kind of protection from competition, at the expense of consumers, in this day and age? My goodness, in Colorado you can smoke pot but you still can't bring your own bottle of wine into a restaurant.

Now to be fair, wholesalers/distributors do serve a vital function. Most retailers and restaurants are not buying huge quantities of wine at one time, nor do they have the temperature-controlled space to store large quantities of wine. Distributors solve this issue by storing wine and delivering it when needed, which is especially important in hot climates, as heat is wine's archenemy. (Even short periods of time exposed to moderate heat can completely destroy the taste of a wine.) The critical thing here, however, is that there's absolutely no reason this distribution function needs to be codified into law. Make it optional and those distributors that do a good job will still have plenty of business, but it would also allow retailers to order wine directly if they so desire, essentially opening up that entire market of 125,000 labels to their customers. As Andrew Murray of Andrew Murray Vineyards stated to me, "Bottom line, it would be a better place if the three tier system was optional . . . not required. The only people it protects are government coffers, cronies, and distributors."

And so I have to ask again: What other industry, besides cable companies perhaps, is allowed to operate this way? (And we all know how much we hate cable companies, right?) In just about every other sector of consumer goods the Internet has helped to do away with protectionist systems like this. Will it happen here? I hope so, and in the meantime if you are within one of the thirty-five to forty states that allow you to buy at least some wine online I encourage you to do it. Not only will you be helping to drive change in the wine industry but you'll also find a vast world of wine way beyond what is normally available in your local market. (For more information on buying wine online see chapter 5.)

TENET #7: LOVE WINE.

For many, myself included, there is a great intimidation factor in wine. However, there is really no reason to be intimidated. I started out knowing nothing about wine. This was also about the same time that the gene I inherited from my father that causes you to progressively lose the ability to pronounce foreign, uncommon, or even common words started to kick in. This is a tough combination for someone venturing into a wine world filled with hard to pronounce names and terms. However, as I've stumbled my way through I've come to realize that the vast majority of people in the wine industry are really fantastic people. This is not to say that the stereotypical wine snobs aren't out there—they definitely are. Luckily they are just a tiny slice of the market and, as you would expect, their snobbiness is not limited to wine. I've come to realize the reason most people in the wine industry are indeed down-to-earth is because, unless you are a very large corporation or a distributor, there's not much money to be made. Ever heard the old joke, "How do you make a small fortune?" The answer: "You start with a large one and then open a winery."

Most small- to medium-size wineries (and some of the large ones) are struggling to survive. Musician Les Claypool said it best in an interview with *Wine Enthusiast* magazine, "Myself and a couple pals said, 'We spend a lot of money on wine, let's make our own, it will be cheaper.' That proved to be one of the most ignorant things that has ever come out of my mouth."[8]

Why would people work so hard at something just to barely stay in business? Because they love it. The wine industry, on the other hand, sometimes makes this hard. Listen, I love wine and I want wine producers to succeed, but in today's world, it's not enough to simply make a good wine; you also need to know your target market and how to reach them. French wine is the perfect example. Everyone knows French wine is some of the best in the world and you don't even need to spend much money on it. But French wine labels are simply the worst. Most of them look the same and all the names start with "Chateau." How in the world do you even remember which one you bought? If the French as a whole were ever able to get their marketing act together, watch out world.

A great example is Beaujolais Nouveau and the huge event that this French region makes out of the new release each year. This is marketing at its best but let's be completely honest—the wine is horrid. Yet they sell an absolute boatload of it because they've turned it into an occasion that people want to be a part of. Just think what these same marketers could do with good wine!

When I visited the Rhone Valley in France recently the wineries there were acutely aware of their deficiencies in this area. Many wineries are changing their ways as the younger generations take

---

8 June 2014 issue of *Wine Enthusiast* magazine.

over the family business. And to be fair, when you sell all the wine you make anyway, why bother? Many regions in Northern Rhone, for example, only have so much space and all of it is already farmed. If there's no way to increase your supply, you'd love to be in the United States but the three-tier system makes it virtually impossible, and you sell out every vintage anyway—what's the point?

To be sure, it's easy to take marketing too far. The large wine corporations love to build wines based on a label or a catchy name. Most of these wines don't actually have a vineyard or even their own wineries. They simply buy bulk grapes and make the wine at the same place as dozens of other labels from the same company. I'm not saying this is necessarily bad; heck, I like some of these wines, but there is certainly something to be said for being authentic and I encourage you to do a little research and seek out wines from small- to medium-size wineries. It may not be easy, as you'll have the three-tier system working against you, but I think you'll find, just like I did, that there's a lot to love.

TENET #8: EVEN THOUGH I LOVE WINE, IT IS STILL JUST A CONSUMABLE.

Wine may not be the equivalent of toilet paper as Annette Alvarez-Peters, the head wine buyer at Costco, so famously suggested in a CNBC special, but it is still a consumable.[9] It's not life or death. You buy it, you enjoy drinking it, and you hopefully repeat at some point in the future. Some people cellar their wine for long periods, but it is only a tiny slice of the market.

As such, don't worry too much about getting the "right" wine. Try a wide variety and you'll soon find what you like. And if you get a bad one, take it back and move on. (Yes, take it back; plenty of stores like Trader Joe's and Costco will happily take returns on opened wine.)

---

9 http://www.cnbc.com/id/46603589

TENET #9: THE WINE INDUSTRY NEEDS TO CHANGE ITS WAYS OR QUIT COMPLAINING ABOUT WINE RATINGS.

The wine industry loves to complain about being constrained by the 100-point scale and other such rating systems. They have a valid point in that many times the focus becomes on the rating, rather than the wine itself. Whether consciously or subconsciously many winemakers chase after a high rating; they try to make wines to fit a particular critic's taste. However, these complaints are completely hypocritical when the wine industry uses those same ratings as their primary marketing tactic.

Look at any wine advertisement in a wine magazine and nine times out of ten, wineries will boast about their 90-point rating from a well-known critic or magazine. (Heck, they even love to plaster it on the bottles themselves.) One of my favorites is when wineries tout their "100-point winemaker," that is, a winemaker who once made a wine that was rated 100 points by a critic—usually from a previous job at a different winery. (Kind of like when an author writes a book that was a bestseller and then slaps the title on five other books after that weren't as stellar.) What's even funnier is when these same wineries loudly exclaim the current hot tagline of how "wine is made in the vineyard." So then why do you need a 100-point winemaker?

Given the wine industry uses these ratings so extensively in their marketing, it's hard to take them seriously when they complain about those very same ratings. The key question for consumers is whether you should pay these ratings any attention at all. I'll be the first to admit that it's hard as a consumer not to fall prey to the allure of a highly rated wine. However, if you've been digesting what we revealed about these wine ratings earlier in this section, you know they are dubious at best. Even with that, I'm not ready to totally discount them—I do think there is a place for wine ratings if, and only if, you can find a reviewer who has similar taste preferences to you. If not, then yeah, wine ratings don't have much purpose. But if you can find a few reviewers who like similar wines it can be a great way to discover new bottles.

TENET #10: PRICE IS IMPORTANT!

We've touched on this in a number of our other tenets, but we highlight it here as well because it simply cannot be said enough. When it comes to wine, price does not equal quality. There's nothing magical about our $20 limit, but it's silly to not bring price into the equation when considering a wine. Most of us are rational human beings who want to get our money's worth out of our purchases. Too many people have allowed themselves to be convinced that price equals quality, which is exactly what most of the wine industry wants you to think. As we discussed in Tenet #4, studies have shown again and again that it simply does not, and this is really what being a Reverse Wine Snob is all about—breaking the price-equals-quality equation and judging wine based on your own preferences.

On a side note, we've found that breaking the high price equals high quality fallacy can be a powerful tactic not just in wine but in other things as well. By flipping this equation on its head you begin to see things in a whole new light, and you also begin to see through the tactics marketers use to try to convince you otherwise. It's a powerful tool to stay on budget in a world of marketers who want anything but that.

CHAPTER 3
WINE TASTING BASICS

WINE IS VERY EXPERIENTIAL. IF you have a nose and a mouth you have everything you need to begin a lifelong discovery process. I wholeheartedly believe the best wine education you can have is through drinking lots of different wines. It can also be helpful to know and understand a few basic wine terms as you begin this journey. Since the next section of our book details many of our favorite wine picks, now is the perfect time to detail a bit of basic terminology you may encounter along the way.

Besides what the wine looks like (the least fun part of the experience) there are three basic parts to tasting a wine:

Aroma/Nose: This is what the wine smells like. The aroma actually contributes to the taste of a wine more than you may expect; much of what we know as taste actually comes from the smells that go through our nasal passages while the food or beverage is in our mouths. We know this intuitively—it's the reason we plug our noses to dull the taste when eating something we dislike and the reason foods just don't have as much taste when we have stuffy noses.

The aromas in wine can also be released and enhanced by swirling it in your glass. We've all seen people do it, and while often thought of as a sure sign of a wine snob, it's actually a very beneficial thing that I encourage you to do. Swirling the wine increases its contact with air, which in turn begins the process of oxidation in the wine—sometimes referred to as letting the wine breathe. As oxygen interacts with the wine different flavors and aromas appear. In many wines, it can be a fascinating thing to smell and taste how the wine changes over the course of a couple hours in your glass. It's easiest to swirl if you put your glass on a flat surface and make small circles until you get the hang of it.

Other common words used when referring to aroma include bouquet and nose.

Taste/Palate: This is the experience of the wine in your mouth—the tastes and textures. There are hundreds of different flavors that can be found in wine, mostly from the grapes, but also from the influence of whatever the wine was aged in (stainless steel, oak, concrete, etc.). You might expect that at some level all wine tastes like grape juice, but fermented grapes result in an amazing array of fruit flavors—blackberry, plum, and cherry are very common in red wines and citrus and tropical fruits are quite common in whites. You may also find more earthy flavors (think mushrooms or vegetable flavors) or even mineral-like characteristics (think of graphite or flinty notes). You may have heard it said that a wine tastes a bit like the soil it was grown in and this indeed seems to be the case in many instances.

Since wine that has aged in oak barrels soaks up some of the flavors from the wood and sap, it is common to find cedar, vanilla, or even chocolate and cinnamon notes in those wines. In addition to these flavors there are several other factors for taste as well:

- The **acidity** level of the wine. That mouthwatering sensation you get from tart foods is an indicator of high acidity. Acidity can help keep a wine fresh and can also help a sweet wine taste less so.
- The **dryness** or **sweetness** of a wine. This is simply an indication of how sweet a wine is and is often measured by the residual sugar in a wine, which is the number of grams per sugar per liter of wine. Generally anything less than 4–5 g/l is considered dry. Some wine producers will include this information on the label, but not many.
- The **body** of a wine (i.e., light, medium, or full-bodied) is basically how "full" the wine feels in the mouth compared to other wines.

- The **complexity** of a wine; in other words, does the wine have lots of different layers and depth, or is it relatively simple and straightforward? If you're constantly finding new flavors and varied nuances to a wine as you drink it, then that's a good indication of complexity. In contrast, a wine that is more one dimensional would be considered simple rather than complex.
- **Tannins** produce a dry, bitter sensation, which doesn't sound that appealing on the surface but can be used to great effect in wine, especially in helping it to age gracefully. Tannins are actually a polyphenol (usually with strong antioxidant properties) that come from contact with the grape skins and seeds during fermentation. (The grape juice's contact with the skins is also where a red wine's darker color comes from.) Oak aging can also impart tannins to a wine.
- The meaning of **minerality** in wine is an oft-debated topic, but I use the term in this book to refer to wines that have stoney, chalky, slate, flinty or salty notes, even if they don't necessarily contain minerals. More often than not these wines have characteristics that one would associate with the soils they are grown in. This is despite researchers' insistence that grapevines cannot take up minerals from the soil, and that many of these minerals have no smell or taste. Yet, somehow, the impression one gets when drinking these wines is unmistakably mineral and so we describe it as such.

Finish: The finish is how a wine ends. It's what happens in your mouth after you swallow. Do the flavors linger? Do they change? The finish is often described in terms of length (short, medium, long) and dryness (your mouth will feel dry after you swallow).

CHAPTER 4

TOP VALUE REGIONS AND VARIETIES

To compile a comprehensive list of wine regions would take a much bigger book than this, and frankly that book has been written many times over. Instead, I have highlighted some of my favorite varieties from some of my favorite areas to get you started on your own exploration of the wonderful world of wine. My list includes regions where you will get the most value for your buck. If you look hard enough you can find quality wines at a low price everywhere, even in a very expensive region like Napa Valley; it may just take some extra work to find them. So pour yourself a glass of wine and enjoy some of my favorite picks! (One additional note: be sure to check the Trader Joe's, Costco, and Box Wine sections later in the book for more great picks from these regions as well as chapter 5: Buying Wine for tips on finding these wines.)

UNITED STATES

When wine from the United States is mentioned, our first thought usually turns to California, but what most people don't realize is that wine is made in the other forty-nine states as well!

California—California is the number one wine producer in the United States. California is best known for Cabernet and Chardonnay but one of my very favorite varieties found here is Syrah. Wine producers throughout the state do an excellent job with this grape, which expresses itself differently in cool climates than it does in hot climates. Tasting a sample from a cool, northern region and then trying one from a hot and dry southern climate and comparing how the same grape ends up in a glass is rather fascinating and insightful.

We'll start our look at California with perhaps my favorite region in the state, Dry Creek Valley in Sonoma. This area is probably best known for its fantastic Zinfandel but it can do a lot more than that, including one of our favorite value varieties, Petite Sirah. If you're a Cabernet lover looking to save money or want a great wine to pair with your steak, Petite Sirah is a great option.

Some of the best value in California comes from blends, a combination of different grape varieties such as Cabernet and Merlot. When done well, these blends allow the winemakers to essentially take the best of each variety and combine them for what is often much greater than the sum of its parts. Many red and white blends in California are terrific.

If you're skeptical of blended wines, just realize this: many of the wines you currently drink from California may be labeled as a single variety but in actuality they are blends! Labeling laws in California (and many other areas) allow a wine to be labeled as a single variety if it contains at least 75 percent of that variety. This means that premium Napa Valley Cabernet Sauvignon that you love (and paid extra for) could have up to 25 percent Merlot in it!

We'll also take a look in this section at one of my favorite types of blends—Meritage. Check out my wine picks to find out just what that is and the correct way to pronounce it!

Washington—The state of Washington is the second largest producer of wine in the United States Wines from Washington are likely to fly under the radar but the state is doing some exciting things with both red and white varieties. Riesling and Merlot are lovely from this region, but thanks to the unique conditions in the state just about every variety thrives there.

Columbia Valley covers 99 percent of the vineyard area in the state of Washington and offers a fascinating study in what wine geeks like to call "terroir." Terroir is a French term associated with wine that means a "sense of place." It essentially refers to the special conditions of a specific place. These conditions can include climate, soil type, and even unique plant characteristics.

In the Columbia Valley the terroir includes conditions like three hundred days of sunshine a year and a desert-like annual rainfall of just 6–10 inches. (This is due to the rain shadow effect from the Cascade Mountains.) The area also boasts a 40 degree diurnal shift, which is the difference between daytime and nighttime temperatures. (Large differences in daytime and nighttime temperatures are wonderful for growing grapes.) Columbia Valley also has extremely unique soil types caused by the Missoula Floods during the Ice Age twenty thousand years ago. These soils allow grapevines to thrive and also impart unique mineral characteristics to the grapes.

Oregon—Oregon is best known for Pinot Noir and they certainly do it well. Lately there have been excellent white wines out of Oregon and just like in California, white blends (combinations of two or more white varieties) offer great value. Oregon also produces everything from Vermentino to Pinot Gris to Albarino to Chardonnay to Syrah to Tempranillo to Riesling and many more. In other words, the state can do much, much more than Pinot Noir.

New York—Whenever I think of wine from New York I can't help but think of the old Pace Picante salsa commercial with the cowboys exclaiming, "That stuff is made in New York City!" Wine may not be the first thing that comes to mind when you think of New York, but areas like the Finger Lakes, the Niagara area and even Long Island are producing great wine. Riesling is at the forefront of this movement, but the region also makes some excellent red wines like Cabernet Franc.

Other highlights—There are many other excellent wine regions throughout the United States, but one of the problems reverse wine snobs encounter is that much of it is above our $20 limit simply because so little is made—there are no economies of scale. Virginia, for example, makes some excellent Viognier and Petit Verdot but the entire state makes as much as wine as one large winery in California! Nevertheless, there is something to be said for drinking local so I do encourage you to check out your local, wineries and give their wines a taste even if they are over $20. If you're in Texas, be sure to check out the good things they are doing with Tempranillo. If you're in Idaho be sure to check out the excellent Riesling. The northern states are doing some really nice things with hybrid grapes designed to survive harsh winters. Even my home state of Minnesota is making some nice wines, including very tasty ice wine.

Delighting in the Dry Creek Valley

Charming, idyllic, and vibrant are just a few of the inadequate descriptors for one of our favorite spots in Sonoma County—Dry Creek Valley.

Located next to the Russian River Valley and the charming town of Healdsburg, the Dry Creek Valley (DCV) is home to over seventy wineries, mostly family owned. The first vineyard was established in 1870 and by the mid-1880s there were over fifty vineyards in operation. But when Prohibition came into place, this long history of grape growing almost ended completely; only four wineries remained after the amendment was repealed in 1933. Much of the former vineyard land in the area was devoted to producing pears and prunes. However, as California wine exploded in the 1970s these farmers quickly realized there was much more

Taking in the sights, smells, and tastes of the Dry Creek Valley.

profit in grapes and the area quickly converted back to grape production. In 1983 Dry Creek Valley became one of the first California wine regions to be recognized as an American Viticultural Area (AVA).

Most probably recognize Dry Creek Valley as the home of fantastic Zinfandel. If you're a fan of this variety, then you no doubt owe it to yourself to check out Zin from this area. But while great Zinfandel may be Dry Creek Valley's claim to fame, this region is no one-trick pony. From surprisingly good Chenin Blanc to old vine Sangiovese, classic Cabernet, fantastic Sauvignon Blanc, to remarkably full flavored Pinot Grigio, and more, we found the quality of wine made in this area to be incomprehensibly good. But be forewarned: if you do visit you may find yourself dreaming of packing it all up, buying a little land, and moving here yourself to grow some grapes (which is exactly the route several of the winery owners we met with took!).

Here is a summary of some of our favorite stops from a recent trip. Most offer very inexpensive tastings (usually $5–$10) and in just about every case the tasting fee is applied to any purchases, making this an extremely affordable trip (unlike some other areas that charge $20–$25 tasting fees that are not applied to any purchases).

GUSTAFSON FAMILY VINEYARDS

The most picturesque setting of all the wineries we visited, Gustafson Family Vineyards is an architect's dream—designed and built entirely from scratch by Dan Gustafson, a landscape architect and real estate developer from Minnesota who decided to make his dream happen in Dry Creek Valley. Back in 2002, while traveling with his family, Dan stumbled upon this 247-acre parcel that had been on the market for four years. While exploring the property, he discovered what might be the biggest Madrone tree in all of California. Remembering that an old-timer once told him that grapes grow best in the same types of soils and conditions as Madrone trees, the rest is history.

Today there are twenty acres of grapes planted: Zinfandel, Petite Sirah, Syrah, Cabernet Sauvignon, Cabernet France, Petit Verdot, Sauvignon Blanc, and Riesling. At 1,800 feet this is the highest elevation winery in Sonoma County. The winery produces about four thousand cases per year. And while it may be a bit off the beaten path, it is worth visiting for the view alone. If you're still not convinced, consider this: the winery sells fruit to Orin Swift Cellars for their renowned wine, The Prisoner. The Gustafson Mountain Cuvée Zinfandel may be the best value we tasted on the entire trip. The Cabernet, Petite Sirah, and Port were excellent as well.

PEDRONCELLI WINERY

One of the originals in the area, the winery is very much a family business run today by brothers John and Jim Pedroncelli. John Sr. started the winery in 1927 (during Prohibition!), using a loan he secured thanks to his service in WWI. Despite what might seem like bad timing, this was actually a good time to grow grapes thanks to a clause in Prohibition that allowed for home winemaking—somebody had to supply those grapes!

We met with Jim Pedroncelli and tasted a number of their wines, all excellent and, better yet, all very affordable. (We've long been a fan of their Petite Sirah.) Eighty percent red, 20 percent white, the winery produces about sixty thousand cases per year. In

addition to the Petite Sirah we loved the Alto Vineyards Sangiovese and of course the Mother Clone Zinfandel, but we were most impressed with the Four Grapes Port, all estate grown using the traditional Portuguese varieties and priced at only $19!

MONICLAIRE VINEYARDS

Sometimes small is better. Moniclaire Vineyards, with a production of just six hundred cases per year, fits that criteria. Winemaker and proprietor Peter Smiderle worked in the semiconductor business before moving to Dry Creek Valley in 1999 with his wife, Mary Beth, and their two daughters, Monica and Claire. Several years later, Smiderle and his family opened up their vineyard. Of course, this wasn't an altogether unexpected venture, as Peter's father and grandfather were both in the wine business.

Today they grow Sauvignon Blanc, Zinfandel, and Petite Sirah, all excellent but the Zinfandel really stood out as an exceptional value. Open only by appointment, I highly encourage visiting. Peter and Mary Beth are fabulous hosts whom my wife and I found both gracious and insightful. After the mad rush at some of the larger wineries' tasting rooms, Moniclaire will be a welcome relief.

RUED VINEYARDS

Owners Richard and Dee Rued are fourth-generation farmers turned vineyard and winery owners. Their land was originally used primarily for prune farming, but in the year 2000, they switched to grapes. Today, they make about three thousand cases per year. All of their wines contains 100 percent of each variety—no blends here. As we've noted before a wine only needs to contain 75 percent of one grape variety to be labeled as a single varietal, so it's quite refreshing to see a winery dedicated to producing 100 percent single varietals—it also lets you experience the true characteristics of each grape, which is quite educational.

The Rueds grow Sauvignon Blanc, Chardonnay, Pinot Grigio, Zinfandel, and Cabernet on their properties, which also include lands in the Russian River Valley and Alexander Valley. In 1881, Richard's grandfather purchased the Russian River Valley property, which was planted to grapes that were changed to orchards after Prohibition. The wines we tasted at Rued were universally good, but the Pinot Grigio in particular was a revelation. This is no typical California watered down Pinot, but one rich and full of flavor—I loved it. If you're a white wine lover this vineyard is a must visit.

DRY CREEK VINEYARD

Dry Creek Vineyard is probably the winery we were most familiar with before our visit because of its excellent Mariner and Sonoma County Meritage wines.

In 1972, David Stare created the first winery in Dry Creek Valley since Prohibition. This winery, which is influenced by both the Loire Valley and Stare's passion for sailing—a fact that is evident in both the architecture and the wine names—has continued to produce fabulous wines for many years. A $12 dry Chenin Blanc was an unexpectedly good find. The Fumé Blanc, which makes up about one-third of its 100,000 case production was also excellent. In fact, David Stare was the first to plant Sauvignon Blanc in the Dry Creek Valley. (Nowadays just about every winery in the DCV has at least some plantings.) On the red side, in addition to the two Meritage bottlings that I love, the Zinfandel and Cabernet offerings were great as well.

FRITZ UNDERGROUND WINERY

Fritz Underground Winery was the first of two wineries we visited that feature wine caves. In this case, the family-owned winery was built underground to conserve energy (there is no heat or air conditioning in the buildings). Extremely picturesque, the setting is just gorgeous.

The wine caves are extremely functional and serve as the perfect spot to age barrels of wine:

While munching on a tasty snack we enjoyed a great value Sauvignon Blanc that flies off the shelves, a surprisingly good Zinfandel Rosé, and once again more simply delicious Zinfandel.

BELLA VINEYARDS AND WINE CAVES

Purchased in 1999 by Scott and Lynn Adams, Bella is a labor of love. After purchasing an existing winery they began a process of replanting as well as adding caves and buildings. Focusing on Zinfandel and Rhone grapes (Syrah and Grenache), all their wines are estate grown and everything we tasted was top notch.

One of the things we enjoyed most about all the wineries we visited in Dry Creek Valley were the fabulous outdoor spaces. Bella is no exception. In addition to wine caves there is a great outdoor gathering spot, perfect for picnics with family and friends. Grab a glass of wine, sit down, and watch your stress level decline.

EVERETT RIDGE VINEYARDS AND WINERY

Everett Ridge Vineyards has a great story—a farming family with four sons who all grew up and established successful careers, and then all came back together to establish one of the very few African American owned wineries in the United States They've had such success that they were recently profiled in the *Wall Street Journal*. They produce Zinfandel, Syrah, and Petite Sirah at Everett Ridge, Cabernet Sauvignon in Alexander Valley, and Pinot Noir and Riesling at their Cole Ranch property, the only single-owner appellation in the United States.

We met with owner Stephen Sterling and winemaker Isabelle Mort to taste several of their wines, including a big meaty Syrah straight out of the tank that showed tons of potential. Their wines tend to be fairly fruit forward with the use of mostly neutral wood that really lets the quality of the grapes shine. Producing about ten to fifteen thousand cases annually, this is another must-visit spot with some excellent Riesling in addition to the very good Syrah, Zinfandel, and Petite Sirah.

SEGHESIO FAMILY VINEYARDS

Last but certainly not least is one of the oldest wineries in the area, Seghesio Vineyards. You probably know this winery for its well-regarded Sonoma Zinfandel, which makes up about 75 percent of its 100,000 case production. What you may not know is the wide variety of other specialized wines it produces. Take for example the fantastic Chianti Station Sangiovese, which comes from the oldest Sangiovese plantings in North America, over one hundred years old, or the Defiant blend featuring Aglianico, Syrah, Petit Verdot, and Cabernet.

In addition to the fantastic wine, the building itself, with its extensive use of reclaimed redwood from the old wine tanks that were shut down with the onset of Prohibition, is a sight to behold. Another special treat at Seghesio is the homemade salami!

Michael David Winery Petite Petit 2010—*Just Plain Fun To Drink*

85% Petite Sirah and 15% Petit Verdot from Lodi, California. 14.5% Alcohol.

Suggested Retail Price: $18. Available for as low as $13.

From the winery:

Loco for Lodi Wine.

Like elephants whose size is imposing, Petite Petit is large! A blend of 85 percent Petite Sirah and 15 percent Petit Verdot, offering a joyous explosion of color and fun! It is a substantial, dense, full-bodied, whopper style of wine loaded with pure black fruit and vanilla flavors that coat the palate. It reveals remarkable richness with a finish that is slightly dry and seems to linger.

One of the best vintages in recent memory, 2010 was a cool, long growing season combined with a medium crop resulting in very balanced and flavorful wines.

Lodi, California, is a great spot for Zinfandel, but what people may not realize is that the variety that often gives Zinfandel its oomph is Petite Sirah. In fact, many wines labeled as Zinfandel have up to 25 percent Petite Sirah. This wine is 85 percent Petite Sirah and a great example of this lesser-known variety that is charming all on its own.

The **2010 Michael David Winery Petite Petit** begins with a very nice aroma of plum, vanilla, lots of spice, and a bit of smoke. The wine tastes fruity without being too sweet and even has hints of vanilla and chocolate. With loads of rich, savory fruit, a nice slightly chewy texture, and smooth but firm tannins this would make a nice BBQ wine—I couldn't help but think it would go well with brats and other grilled fare when I was drinking it.

Taste Rating: 8   Cost Rating: 6

Overall Rating: 7.5

Recommended Buy

MORE RECOMMENDED PETITE SIRAH FROM CALIFORNIA:
- Bogle Vineyards Petite Sirah
- Concannon Conservancy Livermore Valley Petite Sirah
- Pedroncelli Dry Creek Valley Petite Sirah
- Line 39 North Coast Petite Sirah
- McManis Family Vineyards Petite Sirah
- The Crusher Grower's Selection Petite Sirah
- Vigilance Lake County Petite Sirah

Lyeth Meritage 2010—
Make Mine A Meritage

Cabernet Sauvignon, Merlot, Cabernet Franc, Petit Verdot, and Malbec from Sonoma County, California. 13% Alcohol.

Suggested Retail Price: $18. Available for as low as $12.

From the bottle:

Lyeth (pronounced "Leeth") Estates was created 1981 by founder Chip Lyeth, who was captivated by the Bordeaux tradition of blending different varietals to get the most intriguing, inspiring wines. In this spirit, we are proud to offer this original Meritage made in California's Sonoma County. Luscious and full-bodied, it boasts a balanced complexity that only a truly compelling blend can offer.

I'm a big fan of red blends, and one of the more exciting trends to me is the rise of Meritage wines. The term "Meritage" was created in the late 1980's because of a desire to distinguish California wines blended from the traditional French Bordeaux varieties. (The Bordeaux name is, of course, limited to wines that actually come from Bordeaux.) This desire dates all the way back to the infamous "Judgement of Paris" in 1976 when a blind tasting ranked California red and white wines ahead of the very best and most renowned French wines. (Much to the horror of the French, even the French judges chose the wines from California over the ones from France!) Years later, California vintners decided they needed their own term to reflect the high quality of their Bordeaux- style blends, and the term

Meritage was born. Just be sure to say it like an American—think heritage with an M.

This new category seems to have struck a chord with consumers because according to the Meritage Alliance, Meritage has been the fastest growing wine category for three straight years!

Also, just like in Bordeaux, wines must meet certain rules to be called "Meritage." This is regulated by the Meritage Alliance, which began as a California organization but now has members from seven different countries. Regardless of the country of origin, the varieties allowed in red Meritage wines are Cabernet Sauvignon, Cabernet Franc, Merlot, Petit Verdot, Malbec, and Carmenere. Wines must contain at least two varieties, without any comprising more than 90 percent of the total.

The **2010 Lyeth Meritage** begins with pleasing aromas of black cherry cola, raspberry, cedar, and a little chocolate. The wine tastes really excellent with similar flavors as the bouquet. Be sure to give it a little time to breathe—we found it might have even been a little better on day two! Very fruity, nice firm tannins, and a dry finish with good length round out this excellent Meritage blend!

Taste Rating: 8   Cost Rating: 7
Overall Rating: 7.8
Highly Recommended

MORE RECOMMENDED CALIFORNIA MERITAGE:
- Cameron Hughes Napa Valley Meritage
- Cameron Hughes Napa Valley Atlas Peak Meritage
- Dry Creek Vineyard Sonoma County Meritage
- Estancia Reserve Paso Robles Meritage
- Hahn Winery Central Coast Meritage
- Robert Mondavi Private Selection Meritage

Andrew Murray Vineyards Tous Les Jours Syrah 2011—*Another Home Run*

100% Syrah from Santa Ynez, California. 14.5% Alcohol.

Suggested Retail Price: $16. Available for as low as $13.

From the winemaker:
The 2011 vintage is remarkably dark and full-bodied, and yet it has such gentle tannins. It is truly a pleasure to drink, especially at the price. Lots of fruit and spices here . . . no need to wax poetic about this one as it tastes just plain yummy.

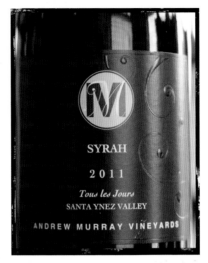

One of the best wines under $20.

We feel the wine makes an ideal "House Wine," the wine you open just for the heck of it, or just to pour a single glass, the rest to be enjoyed later. And at this price, why not? However, we do not skimp on the winemaking for this wine. We start with great grapes from Paso Robles and the Santa Ynez Valley and use the different climates to create a wine that is both fruity and spicy at the same time. I use my experiences with both New World and Old World style winemaking to make the most drinkable Syrah imaginable.

The **2011 Andrew Murray Vineyards Tous Les Jours Syrah** begins with intoxicatingly deep aromas of dark fruit, violets, pepper, mint, and oak. Tasting the wine reveals juicy blackberry and plum interlaced with wonderful peppery spice, fantastic acidity, and savory dried herbs. A bit of earthiness comes out on the long, dry, and very satisfying finish that also features more of that wonderful peppery spice.

What is perhaps most encouraging to me is that as production of this wine has increased (3,900 cases in 2011 versus only 2,200 cases for the 2009 vintage) the quality has not wavered. This also means that the wine appears to be more widely available now than it has ever been.

Taste Rating: 10   **Cost Rating: 6**
Overall Rating: 9.0
Bulk Buy

MORE RECOMMENDED CALIFORNIA SYRAH:
- Bonny Doon Vineyard "Le Pousseur" Syrah
- Brethren of the Road Mendocino Syrah
- Cline Sonoma County Syrah
- Coloma Meatgrinder El Dorado Syrah
- Kendall-Jackson Vintner's Reserve Syrah
- Michael David Winery 6th Sense Lodi Syrah
- Montes Star Angel Paso Robles Syrah

Edmeades Mendocino County Zinfandel 2012—Bring On the BBQ Sauce!

87% Zinfandel, 9% Petite Sirah, and 4% Syrah from Mendocino County, California. 14.7% Alcohol.

Suggested Retail Price: $20. Available at Costco for just $12.79.

From the bottle:

Edmeades is pure Mendocino style. The authentic taste of one of California's final frontiers. Our approach is traditional; our methods are decidedly low tech. We believe in native fermentation in small bins, hand punchdowns and minimal manipulation. With dollops of smoke, graham cracker, chocolate and fruit, it reminds us of raspberry s'mores fresh from the campfire.

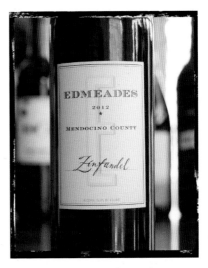

Take your BBQ ribs to the next level.

As much as I complain about the high price of wine at restaurants and the ridiculous rule they use to price a glass of wine at their wholesale cost for the bottle—I still order a glass from time to time. Although it comes at a premium, it lets me try out new wines and new wine/food pairings. That's exactly how I found this wine—when I decided I needed a Zin to pair with my dinner of ribs and rotisserie chicken slathered in copious amounts of BBQ sauce.

The **2012 Edmeades Mendocino County Zinfandel** begins with very pleasant aromas of blueberry and plum along with a little bramble, leather, vanilla, and some excellent smoky notes. This is a really, really tasty wine full of wonderful fruit wrapped up in a smooth and silky texture. Nine months in basically 50 percent French/50 percent American oak (15 percent of which was new) was put to tremendous use here. You'll also be pleased to find notes of cola, leather, and vanilla; soft, fine tannins; and good acidity in this excellently balanced wine. As good as it was with my dinner it was surprisingly just as good on its own. It ends dry and long with more juicy fruit, cola, and lingering vanilla notes. For less than $13 at Costco this might just be my new go-to Zin.

Taste Rating: 9   **Cost Rating: 6**

Overall Rating: 8.3

Bulk Buy

MORE RECOMMENDED CALIFORNIA ZINFANDEL:
- Bianchi Heritage Selection Paso Robles Zinfandel
- Artezin Mendocino County Zinfandel
- Cline Cellars Ancient Vines Zinfandel
- Cline Cellars Lodi Zinfandel
- Four Vines Biker Paso Robles Zinfandel
- Kenwood Jack London Vineyard Sonoma Valley Zinfandel
- Klinker Brick Old Vine Lodi Zinfandel
- Murphy Goode Liar's Dice Sonoma County Zinfandel
- Ravenswood Old Vine Lodi Zinfandel
- Ravenswood Old Vine Napa Valley Zinfandel
- Seghesio Sonoma County Zinfandel

Borra Vineyards Artist Series Kerner Blend 2013— *Truly a Work of Art*

50% Kerner, 25% Riesling, and 25% Bacchus from Mokelumne Glen Vineyards in Lodi, California. 13.7% Alcohol.

Suggested Retail Price: $19. Available at that price.

From the bottle:
Discover the new medium— old world winemaking infused by contemporary label design.

Two rare grapes in one glass.

A place in Europe explained through the eyes of Sheng Moua—a Graphic Design major at the University of the Pacific, in partnership with Borra Vineyards. The first label design in an emerging artist series.

This wine features two cool climate grapes you don't hear much about in the United States. Kerner is a variety that was created in Germany by crossing Schiava (a red grape) and Riesling. Lodi is the only place in California that grows this grape and Borra Vineyards crushed all 4.7 tons that were harvested in 2013.

Bacchus is even rarer in California and is another German crossing of Müller-Thurgau and Silvaner. It is also planted in England, where it is made into a wine reminiscent of Sauvignon Blanc. And while normally you wouldn't think of Lodi, California, as a spot for these cool climate varieties, the Mokelumne Glen Vineyards' placement on the banks of the Mokelumne River creates the cool conditions needed for these varieties to thrive.

The **2013 Borra Vineyards Artist Series Kerner Blend** begins with pleasant aromas of lime, green apple, a little melon and tropical fruit, and beautiful floral notes. Tasting reveals a very fruity wine full of lime and other tangy citrus and tropical flavors. A wonderful light effervescence cranks the refreshment level up another notch. Thanks to all that delicious fruit the wine tastes deceptively sweet, but it is in fact dry. Nice acidity helps to make it very food flexible. It finishes very long.

Winemaker Markus Niggli has nicknamed this wine "Vinho Verde" because he uses the Portuguese style of bottling wine while it is relatively young, which leaves some of the natural carbonation from the winemaking process. It's a good comparison in that those bubbles help create a delicious and refreshing summer wine except that this wine offers a lot more complexity than your average Vinho Verde.

Taste Rating: 9   Cost Rating: 2

Overall Rating: 7.3

Recommended Buy

MORE RECOMMENDED CALIFORNIA WHITE BLENDS:
- Big House White Blend
- Cline Cellars Oakley 82 White
- Conundrum White Wine
- Gnarly Head Authentic White
- Pepi Chenin Blanc Viognier

Pine Ridge Chenin Blanc + Viognier 2013—*A Dynamic Duo*

80% Chenin Blanc from the Clarksburg appellation and 20% Viognier from Lodi, California. 12.5% Alcohol.

Suggested Retail Price: $15. Available for as low as $10 elsewhere.

From the bottle:

A wine often associated with Trader Joe's, but savvy shoppers may want to look elsewhere.

Our distinctive blend marries the crisp, honeyed citrus fruit of Chenin Blanc (80 percent) with the plush body, soft floral and juicy peach notes of Viognier (20 percent) for a lush, versatile and delicious wine. Enjoy a glass on its own or try it alongside your favorite seafood or spicy dish.

Almost all the wines we review from Trader Joe's are exclusive brands that cannot be purchased anywhere else. The reason is simple: Trader Joe's thrives on higher margin private label sales, and not just in wine. It's estimated that over 80 percent of the product they carry is private label. (This, by the way, is totally unlike Costco, which dominates by selling large quantities of mass market brands at extremely low margins.)

The reason these private label products can still be a good deal is simply that Trader Joe's is able to cut out any middlemen and demand super low prices directly from suppliers. On top of that there's also almost no marketing cost (a substantial part of what you're paying for in many products) since Trader Joe's does virtually no advertising.

Widely available products, like today's wine, can be hit and miss at Trader Joe's in terms of pricing. While they are often priced at least somewhat competitively they are rarely at the low end of the market. Such is the case with today's wine, which can be found elsewhere for a couple dollars less. Nevertheless, it's a wine that is often associated with Trader Joe's and I'm guessing they are probably the largest single seller of the eighty-five thousand cases or so produced each year.

The **2013 Pine Ridge Chenin Blanc + Viognier** begins with very pleasant aromas of grapefruit, melon, and pear along with honeysuckle and other floral notes. Tasting the wine reveals loads of juicy succulent fruit of green apple, pear, lots of citrus, and more tropical fruit. The wine also has a fabulous lively acidity and a nice mineral streak that leads into the fresh and tasty finish. This is a fantastic summertime sipper made for hot days on the patio! Also try pairing it with spicy Asian food.

In addition, I also love that the maker of this wine reveals its exact contents. You might think that much like a food, wine should also reveal all of the ingredients used on the label, but this is not the case. In fact, since this wine contains 80 percent Chenin Blanc, the labeling laws in California would have allowed them to label it as just Chenin Blanc with no mention of the 20 percent Viognier it also contains. Kudos to Pine Ridge for the transparency.

Taste Rating: 9   **Cost Rating: 8**
Overall Rating: 8.8
Bulk Buy

MORE RECOMMENDED CALIFORNIA WHITE WINE:

- Bonny Doon Vineyard Central Coast Albarino
- Darcie Kent Gruner Veltliner Rava Blackjack
- Handcraft Chardonnay
- Franciscan Estate Napa Valley Chardonnay
- Line 39 Lake County Sauvignon Blanc
- McManis Family Vineyards Viognier
- Moscato Allegro
- Robert Mondavi Napa Valley Fume Blanc
- Rosa d'Oro Muscat Canelli
- The Independent Chenin Blanc
- Tin Barn Vineyards Sauvignon Blanc
- Uvaggio Lodi Vermentino
- Wente Morning Fog Chardonnay

2010 Bonny Doon Vin Gris de Cigare Rosé—*Fantastic*!

71% Grenache, 16% Roussanne, 11% Grenache Blanc, and 2% Mourvèdre. 12.8% Alcohol.

Suggested Retail Price: $15. Available for around $13.

From the bottle:

> Vin Gris de Cigare is the pink analogue of Le Cigare Volant, our flagship named in honor of the cigar-shaped alien craft banned from landing in the vineyards of Châteauneuf-du-Pape by decree of the village council in 1954. Utilizing prominent Southern French cépages, vin gris is a wine made from the lightest pressings of a noir.
>
> We farm using sustainable practices, with the belief that this discipline is well suited to restoring vital life-forces to our soil and promoting the farm as something akin to a self-sustaining organism. Our winemaking practice is exceptionally light-handed, with minimal intervention and manipulation—unplugged or "acoustic." Equally we are committed to greater transparency. To this end, we append a list of ingredients used in the production of this wine.

As I understand it, this is technically not a true rosé, which is made from red grapes that have minimal contact with the grape skins (and thus the light red color). This wine is made from 71 percent Grenache (a red variety) but also has 29 percent of a Rhone white blend mixed in, a style that's called a Vin Gris. All I know is that whatever style it is, it's fantastic.

The **2010 Bonny Doon Vin Gris de Cigare** has pleasing aromas of strawberry, flowers, and watermelon. The predominant flavors are apple, some citrus, and watermelon but it is not overly sweet and balanced with great minerality and acidity. It ends with a dry, excellent finish. This is an extremely drinkable wine with perfect balance. So crisp and fresh that you could almost guzzle this one on a hot day! I could say more but words don't do this wine justice.

Taste Rating: 9   **Cost Rating: 6**
Overall Rating: 8.3
Bulk Buy!

MORE RECOMMENDED ROSÉ (FROM ALL AREAS, NOT JUST CALIFORNIA):
- Banfi Centine Rosé Toscana (Italy)
- Charles & Charles Rosé (Washington)
- Chateau de Trinquevedel Tavel Rosé (France)
- Cline Cellars Mourvedre Rosé (California)
- Crios Rosé of Malbec (Argentina)
- DeMorgenzon DMZ Cabernet Rosé (South Africa)
- Domaine Houchart Cotes de Provence Rosé (France)
- Douglas Green The Beach House Rosé (South Africa)
- Jean-Luc Colombo Cape Bleue Rosé (France)
- Kanonkop Kadette Pinotage Rosé (South Africa)
- M. Chapoutier Belleruche Côtes du Rhône Rosé (France)
- Las Rocas de San Alejandro Garnacha Rosé (Spain)
- Sorelle Winery Belle E Rosa Lodi Rosé (California)
- Yalumba Y Series Sangiovese Rosé (Australia)
- Zonte's Footstep Scarlet Ladybird Rosé (Australia)

Columbia Crest H3 Horse Heaven Hills Chardonnay 2011—*Cha-Ching!*

100% Chardonnay from Horse Heaven Hills, Washington. 13.5% Alcohol.

Suggested Retail Price: $15. Available for as low as $10.

From the bottle:

Washington State's famed Horse Heaven Hills, named for the wild horses that once roamed this area, have been home to the Columbia Crest winery for over two decades.

Includes an explanation of malolactic fermentation and how those buttery notes get in Chardonnay.

Our winemaker blends innovation and tradition to capture this unique basalt and bedrock terroir creating wines that highlight the intensity of these grapes. This medium-bodied Chardonnay is perfectly balanced delivering aromas of tropical pineapple and pear, flavors of tart apples and caramelized sugar, with a seductive coconut-vanilla finish.

Chardonnay can be a bit of a love/hate proposition for a lot of people mainly because of the two extremes in style that are popular today—the unoaked, fruit forward, high acidity wines typically fermented in stainless steel and the big, rich, oaky, and buttery style popular in California.

It's this second style that people tend to either love or hate. These wines are typically aged in French oak (many times mostly new French oak) and undergo a secondary fermentation called malolactic fermentation. It's this fermentation, and not oak aging, that is actually the source of those distinct buttery notes. A by-product of malic acid (think tart green apple flavors) being converted to softer, creamier lactic acid is diacetyl, which smells and tastes like butter.

The oaky, buttery style is also much more expensive thanks to all that new French oak, which can cost upward of $4,000 per barrel. (American oak is much more economical at $400—500 per barrel.) One barrel only produces twenty-five cases or three hundred bottles of wine, so you can see how quickly these costs add up. Luckily barrels can be used many times, but for a winemaker who wants to utilize mostly new French oak (which will impart the most oak flavors to his or her wine), costs can skyrocket.

And while I tend to prefer the naked or unoaked style, some of my very favorite Chardonnays come from combining the two styles together. The **2011 Columbia Crest H3 Horse Heaven Hills Chardonnay** is one such example. Seventy-five percent of the wine was fermented in a combination of new and used French and American oak and underwent malolactic fermentation. The other 25 percent was fermented in stainless steel and did not undergo malolactic fermentation. The result?

The wine begins with pleasant aromas of citrus, a little vanilla cream, and a little spice. Tasting the wine reveals lots of fruit and a steely minerality that quickly gives way to toasty, oaky, spicy notes that then turn a bit buttery on the finish. This is a rich, medium- to full-bodied wine that offers a great mix of the unoaked and buttery styles in one wine. It ends with long-lasting butter, tobacco, and vanilla notes. This is a great price for a wine of this quality especially when you figure in the cost of those barrels used for 75 percent of the wine!

Taste Rating: 8   **Cost Rating: 8**

Overall Rating: 8.0

Highly Recommended

MORE RECOMMENDED WHITE WINE FROM WASHINGTON STATE:

- Charles Smith Wines Kung Fu Girl Riesling
- Chateau Ste. Michelle & Dr. Loosen Eroica Riesling
- Chateau Ste Michelle Riesling
- Chateau Ste Michelle Dry Riesling
- Long Shadows Poet's Leap Riesling
- Mercer Estates Riesling
- Wysling Band of Sisters White Blend

Bombing Range Red
2010—*A Winning Blend*

56% Syrah, 22% Cabernet Sauvignon, 12% Cabernet Franc, and 10% Mourvèdre from Horse Heaven Hills, Washington. 13.8% Alcohol.

Suggested Retail Price: $16. Available for as low as $12.

From the bottle:

> During WWII our land was used as a training ground for U.S. fighter pilots. The U.S. P-40 Hawk fighter planes depicted on our label capture the spirit of Bombing Range Red, our tribute to U.S. troops and the colorful history of our vineyard.
>
> PHOTO: U.S. P-40 fighter planes at an advanced U.S. base in China. An American soldier waves good luck to the crew. Acme. ca. 1943

Horse Heaven Hills lies within the larger Columbia Valley in Washington and is home to some of the state's oldest vines. It's an extremely dry area, averaging less than ten inches of rain per year. Vitis Vinifera vines, the family of grapes used to make wine, need a minimum of about twenty inches of rain per year to survive, which means that these vineyards almost certainly need to use irrigation to keep their crops alive. The area is also quite hot, although temperatures are regulated a bit by the strong winds.

Dry, hot, and windy normally wouldn't sound like a great combination for farming, but as we touched on earlier these types of challenging conditions help to produce extremely flavorful grapes, just what we want. Many different varieties of wine are grown here in Horse Heaven Hills (so named because an early pioneer called it a horse heaven due to its abundant grasses) and today's wine makes good use of several of them.

The **2010 McKinley Springs Bombing Range Red** begins with pleasant aromas of black cherry, leather, white pepper, and other dried herbs. Drinking the wine shows it to be very tasty with lots of savory fruit and excellent spice that leads into the long fruit- and cola-tinged finish. This is a definite crowd-pleaser from which even the most discerning drinkers will get a lot of enjoyment. A great pick for your Fourth of July BBQ.

Taste Rating: 8   **Cost Rating: 7**

Overall Rating: 7.8

Highly Recommended

MORE RECOMMENDED RED WINE FROM WASHINGTON STATE:
- 14 Hands Winery Hot To Trot Red Blend
- 90+ Cellars Monster Red Blend
- Charles Smith Boom Boom Syrah
- Chateau Ste Michelle Columbia Valley Syrah
- Columbia Crest Grand Estates Merlot
- Columbia Crest H3 Cabernet Sauvignon
- Ex Libris Cabernet Sauvignon
- Hedges Family Estate CMS Red
- Magnificent Wine Company House Red Wine
- Parejas Cellars Tres Rojas de Mesa
- Ridge Crest Cabernet Sauvignon
- Ridge Crest Syrah
- The Keeper Cabernet Franc

2012 Willamette Valley Vineyard Whole Cluster Pinot Noir—*The Whole Story*

100% Pinot Noir from Willamette Valley, Oregon. 13.5% Alcohol.

Suggested Retail Price: $22. Available for as low as $17.

From the bottle:

This whole cluster Pinot Noir was fermented from uncrushed Pinot Noir grape clusters. This technique retains the fresh fruit quality of the varietal and creates a wine which is delicious and accessible upon its release. This wine is an excellent companion with barbecued meats and vegetables, grilled fish, pizza, sushi and spicy Asian Cuisine.

These vines were tended by hand and cluster-thinned to increase flavor and intensity. All of our vineyards are certified sustainable—LIVE (Low Input Viticulture and Enology) and Salmon Safe.

Pinot Noir, a thin-skinned winegrape, develops a natural defense against botrytis (mold) in our moist, cool climate—the antioxidant resveratrol.

Much of the Pinot Noir coming out of Oregon these days goes for over $20, but you really don't have to spend that much to get a delicious and authentic wine. This wine from Willamette Valley Vineyards is a perfect example. For this wine the whole Pinot Noir grape clusters are fermented intact (as opposed to being destemmed and crushed), which essentially means the initial fermentation happens inside each grape. The goal is "to capture pure, fresh-picked Pinot Noir flavors."

The **2012 Willamette Valley Vineyard Whole Cluster Pinot Noir** begins with delightful aromas of wild strawberries and raspberries, spice, earth, and a few white pepper and floral notes. This light- to medium-bodied wine tastes delicious with very light tannins and good acidity. The flavors are similar to the nose but nice and juicy in the mouth, and there is a bit of added cola as well. A smooth and super easy to drink wine that has a lot of character—this isn't a wine you casually sip and then forget about, the memory of it sticks with you! The whole thing might even be a little bit better on day two. I've seen this wine compared in style to Beaujolais, but personally I'd take this over Beaujolais any day.

Also keep your eye out for the smooooooooth **Willamette Valley Vineyard Barrel Select Pinot Noir** at Costco, which generally retails for just under $20. This is a special wine only sold at Costco and was one of the wines that convinced me just how good Pinot Noir under $20 could be!

Taste Rating: 9   **Cost Rating: 4**
Overall Rating: 7.8
Highly Recommended

MORE RECOMMENDED RED WINE FROM OREGON:
- A to Z Wineworks Willamette Valley Pinot Noir
- Abacela Umpqua Valley Tempranillo
- Adelsheim Willamette Valley Pinot Noir
- Argyle Willamette Valley Pinot Noir
- Seufert Winery Syrah
- Seufert Winery Pinot Noir Cuvee
- Stone Wolf Vineyards Barrel Select Pinot Noir Cuvee
- Willamette Valley Vineyard Barrel Select Pinot Noir

Sokol Blosser Evolution White—*A Masterful Creation*

A nonvintage blend of Pinot Gris, Riesling, Muscat, Muller-Thurgau, Gewurztraminer, Chardonnay, Semillon, Pinot Blanc, and Sylvaner from Oregon and Washington. 12% Alcohol.

Suggested Retail Price: $18. Available for as low as $11 at Costco.

From the bottle:

> **Intention**: With over 40 varietals to choose from, what insight led to just the precise amount of 9 of them to form Evolution? Good question.
> Happenstance? Coincidence? Chaos? Not a chance. This bottle you hold is a deliberate, pre-meditated attempt to advance the entire wine universe a notch or two. Grandiose? Perhaps, but without evolution we'd be slime crawling in ooze and that doesn't sound too appetizing.

> **Luck**: Your lucky party . . . EWhite and ERed show up.
> As luck would have it, a random number of varietals took a liking to each other and decided to become a lush, off-dry, somewhat tropical wine with a crisp finish. Go figure.
> Chill. Pour. Sip. Chill. Think about how you might evolve.

I am normally not a big fan of nonvintage wines, which is simply a wine that does not declare the year it was harvested. (In order for a wine to carry a vintage year it must meet certain requirements, mainly that it was actually harvested in that year.) Nonvintage status is fairly uncommon in table wines, but a recent trend among some of the very inexpensive brands is to go nonvintage. The problem with this is that vintage variation is a real thing. Wines can be great one year and so-so (or worse) the next if the harvest is poor. As a result when there's no vintage it becomes hard to recommend a bottle because there's no telling if someone else buying the wine is getting the same thing you tasted.

This wine is an exception because we also enjoy winemakers who don't follow the normal rules. The **Sokol Blosser Evolution White** is what you might call a mega-blend coming from multiple states and, I presume, vintages; however, they also indicate an "edition" so that people like me can rest easy. And just the fact that the wine has been around long enough to have a seventeenth edition is a clue that they are up to something good.

The wine begins with pleasant aromas of citrus, honeysuckle, a bit of tropical fruit, and perhaps a hint of vanilla cream. The wine tastes smooth, crisp, refreshing, and oh so tasty. Deep flavors of citrus, nectarine, green apple, and pear plus a round, soft mouthfeel combine with just the right amount of honeyed sweetness and crisp acidity to make a really delicious and very quaffable wine. Those nine grape varieties add a lot of layers that are quite fun to discover. It ends clean and long. A great wine to pair with spicy Asian dishes.

Taste Rating: 8   Cost Rating: 7
Overall Rating: 7.8
Highly Recommended

MORE RECOMMENDED WHITE WINE FROM OREGON:
- Abacela Umpqua Valley Albarino
- Belle Pente Willamette Valley Pinot Gris
- Bradbourg Gewurztraminer
- Brooks Amycas White Blend
- Brooks Willamette Valley Riesling
- Chehalem Chardonnay
- Soter Brut Rosé
- Troon Vermentino

Red Newt Circle Riesling 2012—*Well-Rounded*

100% Riesling from Finger Lakes, New York. 11% Alcohol.

Suggested Retail Price: $13. Available for as low as $10.

From the bottle:

Versatile, cheap, and delicious—what's not to love?

The Finger Lakes is North America's premier cool-climate winegrowing region. Riesling grapes thrive in the Finger Lakes, producing wines in styles that range from bold, dry and mineral to rich and sumptuous. "Circle" Riesling shows forward fruit flavors of tangerine and apricot with overtones of citrus and honeysuckle. Crisp and slightly sweet, it shows classic Finger Lakes Riesling style and sense of place. It is an exquisite addition to light fare of fruits and cheeses, and is a pleasure to enjoy on its own.

Red Newt Cellars Winery & Bistro is committed to producing exceptional vinifera wines and creating innovative regional cuisine that express the personality and sense of place of Finger Lakes vineyards and communities.

While you may not necessarily think of wine when thinking of New York, maybe you should. New York is the fourth largest wine-producing state in the United States, and thanks to some of the unique micro-climates around places like the Finger Lakes and Niagara Falls, vineyards are able to thrive in this cold climate area. Granted, with a shorter growing season they are more susceptible to bad weather and the consistency from year to year can be harder to maintain, but, as they say, the proof is in the bottle—and this bottle makes a tasty introduction to red from New York.

I'm a big fan of wine from the Finger Lakes and first and foremost among those is Riesling. With 220,000 cases of Riesling produced in the area each year from over 115 different wineries there is a wide breadth of styles made here. For those that are new to this region, this wine is the perfect, well-rounded introduction to Finger Lakes Riesling.

The **2012 Red Newt Cellars Circle Riesling** begins with a very pleasant aroma of apple, pear, honeysuckle, peach, and lime. The wine tastes medium-sweet and exhibits similar flavors to the nose with a touch of added tropical fruit. It also has a wonderful racy texture and good acidity. It ends crisp with good length and lots of lingering honeyed pear and apple notes. Not only is this wine very easy to drink, but it's extremely flexible and will pair nicely with a wide range of foods including spicy dishes.

Taste Rating: 8   **Cost Rating: 8**
Overall Rating: 8.0
Highly Recommended

MORE RECOMMENDED WHITE WINE FROM NEW YORK STATE:
- Billsboro Winery Riesling
- Bouke White Wine
- Hazlitt 1852 Vineyards Riesling
- Heron Hill Winery Ingle Vineyard Riesling
- Fulkerson Winery Semi-Dry Riesling
- Glenora Dry Riesling
- Swedish Hill Dry Riesling
- Three Brothers Zero Degree Dry Riesling
- Wagner Vineyards Dry Riesling

Dr. Konstantin Frank Cabernet Franc 2010—*The Doctor Knows Best*

Cabernet Franc from Finger Lakes, New York. 12.8% Alcohol.

Suggested Retail Price: $20. Available for as low as $16.

From the bottle:
Cabernet Franc, the premier red grape of Bordeaux and the Loire Valley thrives here in New York's Finger Lakes,

where it is considered one of the most promising varieties. In the Dr. Frank's vineyard, it produces small amounts of fruity red wine of medium structure, making it an interesting alternative to more tannic Cabernet Sauvignon.

Dr. Konstantin Frank, known as "the father of Vinifera" in the Eastern United States, pioneered viticulture methods that a generation of Eastern wineries have used to grow these superb varieties of European grapes.

While the Finger Lakes wine region in New York is most known for its excellent Riesling, it's not the only variety that does well in this area, and the Finger Lakes are not all about white wine. Case in point is this Cabernet Franc from the Dr. Konstantin Frank winery. (Cabernet Franc is a major French grape that is one of the parents of Cabernet Sauvignon.)

The **2010 Dr. Konstantin Frank Cabernet Franc** begins with a really pleasant aroma of red and blueberries, spice, and a hint of cedar. The wine tastes super smooth and juicy with flavors of blueberry, plum, oaky spice, and a bit of tobacco. This medium-bodied wine also features good acidity and soft tannins. It ends dry with more savory, juicy, sweet fruit that lingers for a really long time. This is an absolutely delicious wine. And it's another great example of the delicious red wine coming out of New York.

Taste Rating: 9   **Cost Rating: 5**
Overall Rating: 8.0
Highly Recommended

MORE RECOMMENDED RED WINE FROM NEW YORK STATE:
- Arrowhead Red Meritage
- Fox Run Vineyards Meritage
- Fox Run Vineyards Cabernet Franc
- Knapp Winery Lemberger
- Swedish Hill Cabernet Franc/Lemberger

EUROPE

Long thought to be the birthplace of wine, there are literally centuries of winemaking history to explore here.

France—If you asked people to list what comes to mind when they think of France, wine would, without a doubt, be near the top of the list. But there is so much wine that comes from France from so many different regions that it can be dizzingly complex to navigate your way around French wine. Let's take just one of my favorite regions, Côtes du Rhône, as an example.

The most prestigious areas within the Côtes du Rhône are called "Cru." Cru is a French term that translates as "growth." The wines coming from these very specific places are intended to represent the uniqueness of that particular area. Within the Côtes du Rhône designation there are eighteen Crus, broken out into eight Northern Crus in the northern part of the region, eight southern Crus in the southern part of the region, and two Crus for fortified wine that are also in the southern part of the region. In order for wines from these areas to carry the Cru designation they must meet certain standards. In the Rhône Valley these Crus include such renowned growing areas as Côte Rotie, Gigondas, Hermitage, and Châteauneuf-du-Pape.

After the eighteen Crus, the next level down is called Côtes du Rhône Villages. There are a number of villages within in the larger Côtes du Rhône designation that have earned the right to carry this label. Although much of the wine produced here is simply labeled as "Côtes du Rhône Villages," there are eighteen villages that have the right to also include their names on the label due to their special characteristics. These are areas that are basically a half step up from the general Côtes du Rhône Villages designation but not all the way up to the Cru standard. Confused yet?

At the bottom of the pyramid is the basic Côtes du Rhône designation, which accounts for over 50 percent of the production in the Rhône Valley. These are not necessarily lesser-quality wines; in fact, there is a tremendous amount of value to be found in the Côtes du Rhône designation and it is one of my favorite values.

This is just one region in the country! Add in the other fifteen-plus major regions in France, each with its own unique set of rules, and it's no wonder consumers find French wine so confusing. It also doesn't help that most French wines begin with the word "Château" and have rather similar looking labels. In this section I have a number of recommendations to get you started on a life-long journey of exploring French wine.

Spain—It might surprise you to know that Spain has more vine-yard land than any other country in the world. It is also one of our very favorite value regions because so much of that vineyard land is old, which means lots of really old grapevines, which equates to delicious wines.

Spain follows strict laws as to how wineries can label their wine. This means they must meet stringent requirements to get a term like Reserva or Gran Reserva. The region of Rioja, which lays out the following criteria for its wine, is a great example:

- **Young wines:** Wines in their first or second year that keep their primary freshness and fruitiness.
- **Crianza wines:** Wines at least in their third year, having spent a minimum of one year in oak casks and a few months in the bottle. For white wines, the minimum cask aging period is six months.
- **Reserva wines:** Selected wines of the best vintages with an excellent potential that have been aged for a minimum of three years, with at least one year in oak casks. For white wines, the minimum aging period is two years, with at least six months in casks.
- **Gran Reserva wines:** Selected wines from exceptional vintages that have spent at least two years in oak casks and three years in the bottle. For white wines, the minimum aging period is four years, with at least one year in casks.

These requirements mean you have a pretty good indication of what you are getting, and because they require many of the wines to be aged in the bottle for a number of years, the wines are ready to drink when they are released.

Italy—Italian wine is equally as confusing as France, but this is what happens when wine has been made here for hundreds and hundreds of years. Don't let the confusion stop you from exploring this region, however. It is one of our very favorites.

Sangiovese is one of the major grapes in Italy, being the backbone of such renowned wines as Chianti and Brunello di Montalcino, as well as many super Tuscan wines.

A few of the often overlooked areas in Italy, however, may give the best value. For example, Alto Adige in the northern part of the country offers fascinating and affordable wines. Sicily, the largest island in the Mediterranean Sea, likewise offers tremendous value in varieties like Nero d'Avola that you generally don't find anywhere else. Of course we'll also offer some tried and true favorites from places like Tuscany and beyond.

Portugal—The country of Portugal has long been associated with fortified Port wines and for good reason. However, if that's the only wine you drink from Portugal you are definitely missing out. Those same grape varieties used in Port make some of the most exciting red wines on the market. But best of all, none of them will empty your wallet, simply because the region is not as renowned as it should be. Like Spain, France, and Italy, the country has tons of old vineyards with established vines that produce fantastic fruit. Much of the wine made here is happening along the Douro River.

Austria and Slovenia—Austria is probably best known for the white grape, Gruner Veltliner, but it also has its fair share of excellent red varieties that you've likely never heard of: Saint Laurent, Blaufrankisch, and Zweigelt. We also offer a fascinating look into a country right next to Austria, Slovenia, and its unique history as part of Yugoslavia.

Other highlights—This overview of European wine is just scratching the surface. What we didn't mention could fill an entire book itself: Riesling from Germany, Greek wines using native grapes like Xinomavro, and exciting new developments in wine in places like Turkey, Hungary, Bulgaria, and Croatia. It is certainly a great time to be a wine lover!

FRANCE

Pinot Gris from Alsace—*Pinot Grigio that Tastes Good*

Don't get me wrong—there's plenty of good Pinot Grigio out there, but there's also tons of watered down, lifeless "juice" you can barely call wine (California, I'm looking at you). Of course years ago as a very casual wine drinker, I loved the stuff. Give me a bottle of Ecco Domani and I was in heaven. Light as it may be, it's still a fine wine if that's what you're in the mood for. But nowadays, I find myself wanting something with a little more substance and complexity. To be honest, I had just about given up on finding that in Pinot Grigio, except for perhaps the occasional bottle from Alto Adige or Australia. But then I discovered Alsace.

The Alsace region in the north-eastern corner of France is well-known for producing stellar white wines. Riesling and Gewurztraminer are the most popular, but Pinot Gris (aka Pinot Grigio) is a close second. The wines produced here are markedly different than other French wines due to the mixture of volcanic and limestone soils, the unique climate created by the Vosges Mountains and the heavy German influence—this whole region was once under German control. Like any good wine, you almost feel that you can taste these elements in the glass.

Here are four excellent examples of Alsatian Pinot Gris for under $20.

Willm Pinot Gris Reserve 2011—*Definitely Not Your Mother's Pinot Grigio*

Suggested Retail Price: $13. Available for as low as $11. 13% Alcohol.

The wine begins with pleasant aromas of honey-tinged fruit, primarily peach, apricot, and a little pear. Nothing out of the ordinary so far, but it's when tasting the wine you realize that this is not your average Pinot Grigio. The Willm is so much more substantial with a soft and round texture that is really quite pleasing. The wine is modestly sweet but some nice acidity at the core helps to keep the sweetness level in check. It ends with more honey-soaked fruit that lasts for a good, long time in the mouth. This is a great place to start your exploration of Pinot Gris.

Taste Rating: 8   **Cost Rating: 8**
Overall Rating: 8.0
Highly Recommended

Domaine Mittnacht Freres Pinot Gris Les Petits Grains 2011—*Big on Flavor*

Suggested Retail Price: $22. Available for as low as $20. 14% Alcohol.

The Domaine Mittnacht reveals more of the mineral side of Alsace. It begins with peach, apricot, pear, and honeysuckle aromas along with a hint of tropical fruit. Tasting the wine reveals a lovely texture and viscosity with lots of minerals, fruit, and spice. There's also an excellent bright acidity. The fruit flavors are similar to the nose, but the fruit takes a back seat to the minerals and spice when tasting this wine. It ends crisp and clean.

Taste Rating: 9   Cost Rating: 1

Overall Rating: 7.0

Recommended Buy

Domaines Schlumberger Les Princes Abbes Pinot Gris 2009—*Royally Good*

Suggested Retail Price: $20. Available for as low as $15. 13.5% Alcohol.

The Domains Schlumberger begins altogether different than the first two wines. Earthy apple and quince notes, white peach, and hints of smoke and lemon are the first aromas to hit you. That lovely mouthfeel is still there but this time it's rich and even a bit chalky. It tastes similar to the way it smells, but with perhaps a bit more smoke coming through and lasting all the way through to the long finish. What's interesting is that many times a wine with a thick mouthfeel like this would be very sweet, but that's not the case here. And just like the first two wines, lovely mineral notes add intrigue. A wine that just gets better and better with every sip.

Taste Rating: 9   **Cost Rating: 5**

Overall Rating: 8.0

Highly Recommended

Meyer-Fonne Pinot Gris Reserve Particuliere 2009—*Splendid*

Suggested Retail Price: $22. Available for as low as $20. 13.5% Alcohol.

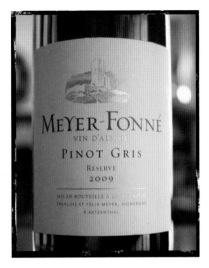

With this wine, the first thing to hit you when smelling it are funky, earthy notes with apple, peach, and a hint of tropical fruit not far behind. The wine tastes absolutely splendid with a lovely and lively texture in the mouth. It isn't at all what I expected from the nose, but it's delicious. Baked green apple, peach, spicy pear, and even a hint of cinnamon combine with good acidity and then eventually give way to chalky mineral notes on the long finish.

Taste Rating: 9   **Cost Rating: 1**

Overall Rating: 7.0

Recommended Buy

MORE RECOMMENDED WINE FROM ALSACE:
- Domaine Jean Ginglinger Pinot Blanc Cuvee George
- Domaine Mittnacht Freres Pinot Blanc Terres d'Etoiles
- Lucien Albrecht Reserve Gewurztraminer
- Lucien Albrecht Reserve Riesling
- Paul Blanck Pinot Blanc d'Alsace
- Trimbach Pinot Blanc
- Trimbach Riesling

Chateau La F leur Morange Mathilde 2010—*Merlot with Moxie*

100% Merlot from Saint-Emilion, Bordeaux, France. 15% Alcohol.

Suggested Retail Price: $19. Available at that price.

From the bottle:

Winelovers worldwide know that over the last decade Saint Emilion has become the unrivaled hotbed of winemaking innovation. This cutting edge wine confirms that trend! From vineyard management to winemaking, the Juliens have pushed the enological envelope.

If people knew Merlot could taste like this, they'd drink a heck of a lot more of it.

From their remarkable 3.3-acre vineyard in eastern Saint Emilion which boasts 50 year old vines, the Juliens manually harvest their fruit at an optimum ripeness in a matter of hours. Yields are tiny and the resulting wine concentrated. It is aged on its lees for 6 months in Taransaud and Darnajou barrels, so as to preserve a maximum of fresh and vibrant fruit. Just 660 cases of this 100 percent Merlot wine were bottled "unfined" and unfiltered in July 2011.

Bordeaux, despite the common perception, is not all about famous producers selling wines at ridiculous prices. In fact, the vast majority of wines made in Bordeaux sell for less than $20, which makes it a great spot for Reverse Wine Snobs looking for deals on tasty wines from established vineyards.

Saint-Emilion, however, is one of the most prestigious areas in Bordeaux and the prices of the wines often show it. The area has a long history of winemaking, going back to Roman times. The most predominant varieties grown here are Merlot (65 percent of the plantings) and Cabernet Franc. This wine actually comes from fifty-year-old vines and offers an amazing price for this area.

One other distinction to note is that the region of Saint-Emilion has four "satellites." These are Lussac-Saint-Emilion, Saint-Georges-Saint-Emilion, Puisseguin-Saint-Emilion, and Montagne-Saint-Emilion. Each covers distinct, small areas bordering Saint-Emilion. Many times, the less expensive wines you see will come from one of these appellations, but this wine does not.

The **2010 Chateau La Fleur Morange Mathilde** begins with a wonderful and complex aroma featuring dark fruit, licorice, spearmint, earth, cola, and a little vanilla. Wow, this wine tastes delicious with tons of jammy fruit but this is no one-trick wonder. Many of the other flavors from the nose carry over as well—licorice, earthy notes, and cola in particular, plus you'll find some added cedar, cocoa, and tobacco. There is also wonderfully integrated spice notes, great acidity, and a lush, smooth mouthfeel. It ends dry with good length.

Another hint to make your way through the maze of Bordeaux wines is to look for the Bordeaux Superieur designation, which is exactly as it sounds—a label given to wines that have slightly more stringent production regulations than the regular Bordeaux wines. This doesn't always translate into a better wine, but generally the quality should be slightly higher as the Bordeaux Superieur wines tend to come from older vines with lower yields and they spend more time aging before their release.

Taste Rating: 10   **Cost Rating: 2**

Overall Rating: 8.0

Highly Recommended

MORE RECOMMENDED WINE FROM BORDEAUX:
- Chateau Bonnet Reserve Bordeaux Rouge
- Chateau Bourbon La Chapelle
- Chateau Cote Montpezat Cuvee Compostelle
- Chateau de Sours Rosé
- Chateau des Landes Lussac-Saint-Emilion
- Chateau Jean Faux Sainte-Ragonde Bordeaux Superieur
- Chateau Le Thil Comte Clary Blanc
- Chateau Mayne Guyon
- Chateau Rollan de By Cru Bourgeois Medoc
- Chateau Saint Julian Bordeaux Superieur
- Mission Saint Vincent Reserve Bordeaux Rouge
- Lestonnat Bordeaux Superieur

Cameron Hughes Lot 354 Crozes-Hermitage 2010— *Get It While You Can*

Syrah from Crozes-Hermitage, Rhone, France. 13.5% Alcohol.

Suggested Retail Price: $20. Available for just $10.99 at Costco. Only 2,400 cases produced.

From the bottle:

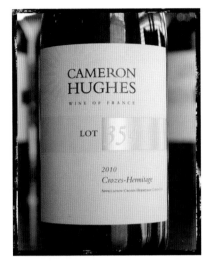

Cameron Hughes is an international négociant, sourcing and producing small lots of high quality wine from the world's best regions. Cameron

Crozes-Hermitage at half the price thanks to Cameron Hughes and Costco.

offers a diverse range of wines uniquely represented by the Lot number on this label.

Lot 354 is ripe and concentrated with notes of black cherry, plum paste and violet. Rose petals and fresh woodland berries contrast the monumental texture. Outstanding.

Crozes-Hermitage is located in the Northern Rhone Valley in France. The region is known for its excellent Syrah-based wines, and while not as prestigious as the Hermitage appellation that it surrounds, the wines often command a premium. Finding a bottle of this quality for $11 is quite the score, which means this inventory will get snapped up fast. In other words, if you're lucky enough to see it make sure you grab a bottle straight away.

The **2010 Cameron Hughes Lot 354 Crozes-Hermitage** begins with very pleasant aromas of blackberry, plum, a really nice earthy streak, a little spice, and pepper. Tasting delights with tons of delicious dark ripe fruit infused with lovely pepper and spice.

The earthy notes from the nose also carry over in this beautifully balanced wine. Even better, the whole thing is enveloped in a wonderful deep, dense, and chewy texture. It finishes quite long. Sure to move fast, so get it while you can!

Taste Rating: 9   **Cost Rating: 7**

Overall Rating: 8.5

Bulk Buy

MORE RECOMMENDED WINE FROM THE RHONE VALLEY:
- 90+ Cellars Lot 30 Côtes du Rhône
- Andezon Côtes du Rhône Red
- Chateau de Clapier Rosé
- E. Guigal Crozes-Hermitage
- Jean-Luc Colombo Les Abeilles Blanc
- Jean-Luc Colombo Les Abeilles Rouge
- Lavau Côtes du Rhône
- M. Chapoutier Côtes du Rhône Belleruche Rouge
- M. Chapoutier Côtes du Rhône Belleruche Rosé
- Vidal-Fleury Côtes du Rhône Rouge

Paul Mas Estate Single Vineyard Collection Malbec 2011—*A Throwback*

100% Malbec from Pays d'Oc AOP, Languedoc, France. 13.5% Alcohol.

Suggested Retail Price: $14. Available for as low as $12.

From the bottle:
Paul Mas Estate Single Vineyard Collection wines come from Jean-Claude Mas's vineyards in the Languedoc region in the South of France.

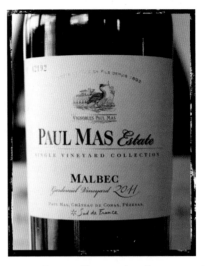

Before Malbec made it big in Argentina it thrived in France.

Gardemiel (which means the place where the honey is kept) is located at 200 km from Cahors, historical birthplace of Malbec grape variety, and 12,000 km from Argentina, where it became the icon grape of the country. In our picturesque vineyard, at the foothills of the Pyrenees mountains, our malbec has a unique profile, with its dark colour, its nice acidity combined with softness, its ripe berry flavours and liquorice notes. This is pure French appeal!

While today Malbec is usually used as a blend component in France, it used to be grown all over the country. It lost popularity with many grape growers in 1956 when a seriously bad frost killed off up to 75 percent of the plantings in some areas. Argentina is the new Malbec king, but don't write off France too quickly. In areas in France where Malbec is still made into a single varietal wine, you can find some absolute gems.

The **2011 Paul Mas Estate Single Vineyard Collection Gardemiel Vineyard Malbec** begins with a tantalizing and complex aroma of black cherry, red licorice, juniper, plum, prune, and dried herbs. The wine tastes smooth and delicious with lots of rich, tart fruit along with great balance and structure. This shows a great counterpoint to Argentinean Malbec with tons of complexity and depth. Its succulent dried herb component along with some nice earthy notes lead into the long finish.

Taste Rating: 9   Cost Rating: 7

Overall Rating: 8.5

Bulk Buy

MORE RECOMMENDED WINE FROM THE REST OF FRANCE:
- Arrogant Frog Pinot Noir
- Bouchard Aine & Fils Chardonnay Vin de Pays d'Oc
- Bouchard Aine & Fils Pinot Noir Vin de Pays d'Oc
- Cave de Lugny Charmes Chardonnay
- Chateau Paul Mas Clos des Mures
- Domaine du Tariquet Classic Cotes de Gascogne
- Fortant Coast Select Grenache Rosé
- Georges Duboeuf Morgon Domaines des Versauds Beaujolais
- Gerard Bertrand Grand Terroir Tautavel
- Guy Saget La Petite Perriere Sauvignon Blanc
- Henry-Fessy Beaujolais-Villages
- Jean-Luc Colombo Cape Bleue Rosé
- Joseph Drouhin Laforet Bourgogne Chardonnay
- Joseph Drouhin Laforet Bourgogne Pinot Noir
- Locations F-2 French Red
- Shatter Grenache
- Villebois Sauvignon Blanc

Bodegas Filon Garnacha 2011—*Crazy For The Calatayud*

100% Garnacha from Calatayud, Spain. 14.5% Alcohol.

Suggested Retail Price: $10. Available widely for $8.

From the bottle:
> The incredible composition of land that make up the slopes of many hills in the district of Calatayud, in most cases covered with slate and very poor in nutrients, allowing the cultivation of vineyards that produce wonderful grapes Grenache, which gives highly concentrated and elegant wines with aromas reminiscent of cherries and black plums.

It's hard to believe this wine is only $8.

We've said it before and we'll say it again. We're simply crazy for the Calatayud region in Spain. In fact, with tons of delicious wine made from old vine Garnacha for well under $15, this may be one of the best value locations in the whole world.

The unique environment of high altitudes, rocky soils, and lots of sunlight sets Calatayud apart from many other wine regions. All of these factors, plus the very old age of the vines, means you're looking at low grape yields, which you might think to be a bad thing. But in the world of wine low yields are a very good thing because they equal more flavorful fruit. As a general rule, the harder it is for the grapevines to grow, the more flavorful the grapes. And because there are a number of these old vineyards around and the area is not as well-known as many others, the prices we pay do not come anywhere close to reflecting the true value of these wonderfully old vines.

The **2011 Bodegas Filon Garnacha** begins with a very pleasant aroma of menthol, black cherry, and a bit of smoke. The wine tastes smooth, supple, and harmonious. The dark, rich fruit, cola, spice, and mineral notes just flow together perfectly. The savory flavors continue on the long finish and are joined by some nice spicy mineral notes and a hint of smoke that lingers in the mouth for a good time.

Taste Rating: 9　　　**Cost Rating: 9**

Overall Rating: 9.0

Bulk Buy

MORE RECOMMENDED WINE FROM THE CALATAYUD:
- Altovinum Evodia Old Vines Garnacha
- Atteca Old Vines Garnacha
- Bodegas Breca Old Vines Garnacha
- Cruz de Piedra Garnacha Tinto
- Las Rocas Garnacha
- Punto y Coma Garnacha
- The Show Garnaca

Albarino—*Made For Summertime Sipping on the Patio*

Albarino, an often overlooked variety, is one that should definitely be on your get-to-know list. Why? Let me put it this way . . . if Spain, which has more vineyard land than any other country, chooses Albarino as one of the very few white varieties that it produces and labels as a single varietal, there just might be something special here.

Albarino Quick Facts:

- Accounts for 90 percent of the grapes grown in Rias Baixas (ree-ahs-buy-shuss), Spain.
- Also produced in Portugal where it is called Alvarinho and often used in the delicious Vinho Verde wines.
- Usually fermented in stainless steel, which produces a lighter bodied wine, but barrel fermentation and oak aging are also occasionally used to produce a fuller wine.
- Many times produced slightly effervescent, or frizzante.
- A low-yielding variety that is expensive to cultivate.
- A great match with seafood.

Of course the best way to experience Albarino is to taste it, so I encourage you to seek it out. Here are three selections to get you on your way.

First up is the 2011 Pazo Torrado Albarino

100% Albarino from Rias Baixas, Spain. 12.5% Alcohol.

Suggested Retail Price: $15. Available for as low as $13.

From the bottle:

Pazo Torrado is a 100 percent Albarino wine from the Salnes Valley belonging to the Rias Baixas Designation of Origin in Galicia. The camelia flower on the label, symbolizes the freshness and floral beauty of this wonderful Albarino, with aromas of citrus and tropcial fruit flavors.

The **2011 Pazo Torrado Albarino** begins with a salty, green apple aroma with complementary floral notes. Tasting the wine reveals a lively texture with fresh acidity and lots of lime, green apple, and citrus flavors. This is a pure and refreshing wine. It ends with a nice clean finish and good length. It's both easy to drink and interesting—two things that don't always go together.

Taste Rating: 8   **Cost Rating: 6**

Overall Rating: 7.5

Recommended Buy

Our second pick is the 2011 Adega Pazos de Lusco Albarino.

100% Albarino from Rias Baixas, Spain. 13% Alcohol.

Suggested Retail Price: $22. Available for as low as $19.99.

From the bottle:
> A Pazos de Lusco was founded in 1996 upon acquisition of the historic Pazo Pineiro estate, a 12 acre property offering ideal growing conditions for the spectacular, aromatic Albarino grape variety. Lusco, the result of superb fruit and natural wine-making, offers concentration and elegance on a par with the world's finest dry white wines.

The **2011 Lusco Albarino** begins with pleasing aromas of pear, a little citrus, sea salt, and a hint of lemon custard. Tasting the wine reveals a substantial mouthfeel with a nice zestiness to it. You'll also find lots of citrus and mineral notes plus a little tropical fruit that builds into the finish. This is a bigger wine than the Pazo Torrado, with everything amplified a bit. On the finish the tart tropical fruit continues for a surprisingly long time and a bit of lemon custard from the nose reappears.

Taste Rating: 9   **Cost Rating: 1**

Overall Rating: 7.0

Recommended Buy

Our third pick is the 2013 Paco & Lola Albarino.

100% Albarino from Rias Baixas, Spain. 12.5% Alcohol.

Suggested Retail Price: $20. Available for as low as $12.

From the bottle:
Variety: 100 percent Albariño sourced from the winery's own vineyards.

Fermentation: fermented in stainless steel vats, with temperature controlled.

A love story.

Appearance: attractive straw color with hints of green in the rim. Clean and brilliant.

Nose: very expressive and harmonious nose. Fine notes of white fruit (green apples, pear) and lemony aromas. Hints of herbs (basil) and flower blossom base notes. Surprising aromatic intensity.

Palate: fresh with good structure and the same fruit characters as found on the nose. Slightly balsamic finish.

Paco & Lola make a Divine Duo with sushi, pastas, fish, rice dishes, white meats, seafood, fish and shellfish stews.

The **2013 Paco & Lola Albarino** begins with pleasant notes of pear, peach, apple, a little tropical fruit, and light floral and herbal notes. The wine tastes really delicious with refreshing tangy citrus and tropical fruit. It also has good acidity, a lively and silky texture, and excellent touches of sea salt minerality. It ends with good length, lemon, and more sea salt minerality. This is a major quaffer that still has pretty good complexity.

Taste Rating: 8   **Cost Rating: 7**

Overall Rating: 7.8

Highly Recommended

MORE RECOMMENDED WINE FROM RIAS BAIXAS:

- Bodegas Fillaboa Albarino
- Licia Albarino
- Salneval Albarino
- Valminor Albarino

Reveling in the Wine of Ribera Del Duero with Two Top Value Picks

Ribera Del Duero sits on the northern plateau of the Iberian Peninsula and literally means "banks of the Douro," referring to the river that splits the region and supplies much-needed water to the area. This is the same river that flows through Douro and Porto in Portugal, which makes you wonder if there's something magic in the water! The soil in the area is clay—there's really no topsoil at all.

Perhaps the biggest challenge to growing grapes here is the lack of moisture in the winter. And what a winter it can be, hitting 10 degrees below zero. Combine that with temperatures approaching 105°F in the summer and you have one extreme climate. Despite the extreme temperatures, the area, which sits at about 2,800 feet above sea level, offers that magical combination for grapes—hot days and cool nights.

Ribera Del Duero produces Tempranillo almost exclusively. (The local name for the Tempranillo grape is Tinto Fino or Tinta Fina.) There is very little to no white wine production, although there is one white grape grown here called Albillo, which is sometimes blended in very small quantities into the red wines. Speaking of the red wines, they must contain at least 75 percent Tempranillo, although most contain at least 90 percent. Cabernet Sauvignon and Merlot, usually make up the additional 10 percent but Garnacha, Malbec, and the aforementioned Albillo occasionally show up.

The aging requirements for wine in Ribera Del Duero are the same as Rioja, with Crianza, Reserva, and Gran Reserva designations. In other words, much of the wine produced here is built to age, and that it does quite well.

Our first pick is the 2011 Bodegas Barco de Piedra Tempranillo.

100% Tempranillo. This delicious wine can be found for as little as $10. 13.5% Alcohol. The wine features deep, dark, and rich fruit with a smooth, full texture. This is a great example of a lightly oaked Tempranillo that proves the wine can still be robust and powerful without spending a long time in barrels. It ends nicely with spicy mineral notes and more dark fruit that sticks around for a long time.

Tastes like a lot more than $10!

Taste Rating: 8   **Cost Rating: 8**

Overall Rating: 8.0

Highly Recommended

Our second value pick is the 2009 Seleccion de Torres Celeste Crianza.

100% Tempranillo with an SRP of $28. 14% Alcohol. Lucky for us, it can be had for around $17. The Celeste begins with a really lovely and expressive nose of dark fruit (blackberry, black cherry, black currant) as well as some vanilla. This medium- to full-bodied wine tastes simply succulent with lots of juicy fruit and a smooth texture. Beware, however, that if you simply pop and pour this wine you're likely to be disappointed; rather, let it breathe and you will surely be rewarded. It also has some relatively big tannins that I love. This is a wine you can easily cellar for a few years and it will only get better. It finishes dry with tart, lip-smacking fruit flavors and good length.

Heavenly.

Taste Rating: 10   **Cost Rating: 4**

Overall Rating: 8.5

Bulk Buy

MORE RECOMMENDED WINE FROM RIBERA DEL DUERO:

- Bodega Matarromera Crianza
- Bodegas Cuevas Jimenez Ferratus A0
- Condado de Haza Crianza
- Emilio Moro Tempranillo
- Legaris Crianza Tempranillo
- Protos Tinto Fino
- Valduero Crianza Tempranillo
- Vinedos Alonso del Yerro

Vina Eguia Rioja Reserva 2007—*Run, Don't Walk to Get This Wine!*

100% Tempranillo from Rioja, Spain. 13.5% Alcohol.

Suggested Retail Price: $25. Available at Costco for the incredible price of only $10!

From the bottle:
> Made from selected Tempranillo grapes from our best vineyards. After a temperature controlled fermentation, 24 months ageing in American and French oak barrels and final process of bottle maturation in our cellars, we attain this fine and balanced wine.
>
> Bright cherry red in colour. Displays a deep complexity of ripe red fruits, spices, tobacco and liquorice very well balanced. Warm, complex and elegant in the palate with a long and velvety aftertaste. Ideal to serve with all types of meat dishes, stews and matured cheese.

I stumbled upon this wine on a trip to Costco. As I perused the store, I pulled out a $10 bottle to take a closer look and was shocked to find a 2007 Rioja Reserva. At $10, it seemed too good to be true. Rioja has very strict standards for labeling their wine and a Reserva wine must be aged for at least twelve months in oak and then another twenty-four months in the bottle. This wine was aged for twenty-four months in oak and then another twenty-four months in the bottle. Oak barrels can be incredibly expensive, so when you factor in twenty-four months spent in oak and another two years of storing the wine in bottle after that, it's almost shocking that it could be priced so low. Let's just say I was way too intrigued to pass this one up.

Upon returning home I did a little research and found that the popular website Wine Enthusiast rated this wine #18 on its top 100 list for 2011. Mind you, this was not a budget list but the overall top 100 with wines of all price points. I generally don't put a lot of stock in these lists, but this certainly piqued my interest even more.

The oak influence on the **2007 Vina Eguia Rioja Reserva** is apparent but there's also strong vanilla aroma and notes of black cherry, spice, and licorice, which all become more prominent as the wine opens up. Tasting the wine also shows lots of oak influence in the strong vanilla flavors, but again the fruit appears nicely with some air. The wine has strong and rich tannins and a nice dense mouthfeel. Patience is definitely rewarded here because as it breathes you gets loads of licorice, cola, black cherry, and mixed berries along with vanilla and cinnamon. The medium-long finish is dry and has slightly sour black cherry cola and vanilla flavors.

It's pretty rare you can find an age-worthy gem like this for only $10. I liked it so much I hurried back to Costco first thing the next morning to stock up! Already quite good now, in a couple more years, this wine will be utterly fantastic.

Taste Rating: 9   **Cost Rating: 8**
Overall Rating: 8.8
Bulk Buy

MORE RECOMMENDED WINE FROM RIOJA:

- Bodegas Beronia Rioja Reserva
- Bodegas Ondarre Reserva
- Bodegas Montecillo Reserva
- Bodegas Montecillo Gran Reserva
- Campo Viejo Rioja Tempranillo
- Castillo Labastida Crianza
- CVNE Cune Reserva
- Marques de Vitaria Gran Reserva
- Palacios Remondo La Vendimia
- Rio Madre Rioja Graciano
- Valduero Crianza Tempranillo
- Vinal Pomal Crianza
- Vino Zaco

2010 Ochoa Moscatel De Grano Menudo—*500ml*
Never Went Down So Easy

A sweet dessert wine of 100% Moscatel from Kingdom of Navarra, Spain, in a 500ml bottle. 12.5% Alcohol.

Suggested Retail Price: $20. Available at that price.

From the bottle:
> The grapes are grown at the higher levels of our Traibuenas Vineyards, the Ochoa Moscatel a petit grains is collected slightly over-ripe, with a great concentration of sugars, flavor and aromas. It is a light, fragrant, elegant wine with intensely ripe fruit.

The Kingdom of Navarra is an autonomously ruled region in Spain (kind of like Texas) with a history going back 1,200 years. It was originally the Kingdom of Pamplona. Navarra is also a limited wine zone within the Kingdom between Rioja and Bordeaux that grows a surprising variety of grapes.

The **2010 Bodegas Ochoa Moscatel de Grano Menudo** begins with aromas of grapefruit, peaches, and even a bit of almond. The wine is syrupy sweet and tastes of peaches, apricots, lime, and honeysuckle. This is a *very* drinkable wine and once you start you likely won't want to stop. The finish has a nice acidity to balance out the sweetness. This wine was just as good on day two, but I'm betting it'll never make it that long. It pushes the limit of our price boundary, but this a great wine to splurge on for your next dinner party!

Taste Rating: 9   Cost Rating: 1

Overall Rating: 7.0

Recommended Buy

MORE RECOMMENDED WINE FROM THE REST OF SPAIN:
- 90+ Cellars Lot 114 Toro
- Alto Cinco Garnacha
- Beso de Vino Old Vine Garnacha
- Bodegas Peique Ramon Valle
- Borsao Berola
- Borsao Tres Picos Garnacha
- Cyan La Calera Toro
- H&G Priorat Red
- Los Dos Grenache + Syrah
- Marques de Riscal Rueda
- Mas de Leda Tempranillo
- Scala Dei Priorat Prior
- Sicoris Costers del Segre
- Tarima Monastrell
- Yaso Toro
- Zestos Old Vine Garnacha

Cantina Terlano Pinot Bianco 2010—*Something Special from Alto Adige*

100% Pinot Bianco from Alto Adige, Italy. 13.5% Alcohol.

Suggested Retail Price: $21. Available for as low as $15.

From the winery:

Made from Pinot Bianco grapes grown on the porphyric-gravel slopes of the Classico region. Fermentation takes place in temperature-controlled stainless steel tanks

Refreshingly complex.

and the wine rests on the lees for 6 months before release.

With wonderful aromas of apple cider, chalk and lemon zest, this clean and focused wine expands on the palate to reveal warm apple crisp, clove and quince nuances. Possessing a long, concentrated citrus finish, this wine pairs perfectly with roasted pork, shellfish and egg-based sauces or as a charming cocktail beverage.

This wine is from one of our favorite areas, Alto Adige. This area reminds me a lot of Alsace, France, in that both areas have significant mountain influence and the melding of more than one culture—Italy, Germany, and Austria in the case of Alto Adige; France and Germany in the case of Alsace.

Both areas also produce deliciously complex white wines unlike almost anywhere else in the world. They take what can be humdrum varieties elsewhere (like Pinot Grigio and Pinot Bianco) and turn them into something special.

The **2010 Kellerei-Terlan Cantina Terlano Pinot Bianco** begins with pleasing, fragrant aromas of apple, pear, chalk, and a little honeysuckle. Tasting the wine reveals a really nice spicy mineral streak on top of a wonderful, complex mouthfeel. Lush flavors of tart apple, pear, and melon combine with a bright acidity in the mouth. Chalky minerals and citrus zest reveal themselves on the medium-long finish.

Taste Rating: 9   **Cost Rating: 5**

Overall Rating: 8.0

Highly Recommended

MORE RECOMMENDED WINE FROM ALTO ADIGE:
- Castelfeder 15 Pinot Grigio
- Cavit Alta Luna Phases Red
- Colteranzio Weisshaus Pinot Bianco
- Erste + Neue Weissburgunder-Pinot Blanc
- Mezzacorona Teroldego Rotaliano
- Mezzacorona Pinot Noir Riserva
- Nals Margreid Penon Pinot Bianco
- Nals Margreid Galea Vernatsch Schiava
- San Pietro Lagrein
- Tiefenbrunner Turmhof Lagrein
- Tramin Lagrein

Donnafugata Anthilia Sicilia Bianco 2011—*A Succulent Sicilian*

Indigenous Sicilian grapes Catarratto and Ansonica (Inzolia) plus other international varieties like Chardonnay and Viognier from Sicily, Italy. 12.5% Alcohol.

Suggested Retail Price: $15. Available for as low as $12.

From the bottle:
> Our family has crafted wines in Sicily for 150 years. Anthilia is a friendly, fruit-driven wine, crisp and versatile.

This wine comes from Sicily, which surprisingly (to me at least) accounts for almost 20 percent of Italy's total wine production. This doesn't necessarily sound huge until you realize that it translates to more vineyard land than either Chile or South Africa have (as well as more than any other region within Italy). And of these vast Sicilian vineyards the acres devoted to the Catarrato grape account for about one-third. (Nero d'Avola is the second most produced grape, and top red.) Much of the Catarrato that is produced is blended with the white grapes Inzolia and Grillo to make the famous wine Marsala, a fortified wine similar to Port, but lucky for us a growing amount of these indigenous grapes are being used to produce excellent and affordable everyday wines.

The **2011 Donnafugata Anthilia Sicilia Bianco** begins with a nice crisp and fruity aroma of green apple, pear, peaches, and a little grapefruit. Tasting the wine reveals a nicely tart combination of green apple, a little grapefruit, pear, and creamy lemon/lime zest. This delicious wine has a great lively yet soft texture, good acidity, and excellent underlying minerality. On the long finish that minerality turns chalky and comes to the front.

Taste Rating: 8   **Cost Rating: 7**

Overall Rating: 7.8

Highly Recommended

MORE RECOMMENDED WINE FROM SICILY:
- Costa Pietra Nero d'Avola
- Donnafugata Lighea Zibibbo Sicilia
- Donnafugata Sedara
- Lagaria Syrah-Nero d'Avola
- Planeta Cerasuolo di Vittoria
- Purato Nero d'Avola
- Tasca d'Almerita Regaleali Bianco Sicilia
- Valle dell'Acate Il Frappato Vittoria

Frescobaldi Nipozzano Chianti Rufina Riserva 2009—*Love at First Sniff*

90% Sangiovese and 10% other varieties (Malvasia Nera, Colorino, Merlot, and Cabernet Sauvignon) from Chianti Rufina, Tuscany, Italy. 13.5% Alcohol.

Suggested Retail Price: $22. Available for as low as $17, including at Costco.

From the bottle:

> Built in the 11th century, Castello di Nipozzano is located in the foothills of the Apennine mountains, in Tuscany's acclaimed Chianti Rufina growing zone. It is the historic estate and home of the Frescobaldi family.

I'm crazy for Chianti. The tart cherry flavors, the excellent acidity, and the rough edge all combine to make a wine with a lot of character—something that seems to be lacking in many mass produced wines today. There's definitely something to be said for being distinctive in a wine world where too many producers strive to produce the same French Oak-ed, high alcohol, fruit bombs.

I walked by this wine a number of times at my local Costco, and was frequently tempted to buy it. *But I have so much Chianti already,* I thought, *I just can't justify another bottle.* But the classy label, the sub-$20 price point, the high scores, and the rave reviews from others I admire made it impossible to ignore any longer.

The **2009 Marchesi de Frescobaldi Nipozzano Chianti Rufina Riserva** begins with a really lovely, strong aroma of black currant, leather, dried herbs, menthol, cranberry, and wild berries. Tasting the wine reveals fantastic sour berry and apple, lots of dried herbs just like the nose, and a little black pepper. This wine has a smooth and silky texture but still retains the signature rough edge of a good Chianti. Sweet and chewy tannins lead into the very long finish and those dried herbs show up again and linger in the mouth for a long time—so much so that you can almost taste those rustic Italian dishes this wine would pair so well with. Yum!

Taste Rating: 10   **Cost Rating: 4**
Overall Rating: 8.5
Bulk Buy

MORE RECOMMENDED CHIANTI:
- Banfi Chianti Classico
- Banfi Chianti Superiore
- Basilica Cafaggio Single Estate Chianti Classico
- Castello Di Farnetella Chianti Colle Senesi
- Coltibuono Cetamura Chianti
- Cecchi Chianto Classico
- Cecchi Natio Chianti
- Colognole Chianti Rufina
- Falchini Titolato Colobaia Chianti Colle Senesi
- Fattoria Lavacchio "Cedro" Chianti Ruffina
- Il Molino di Grace Chianti Classico
- Piccini Chianti Classico
- Rocca di Castagnoli Chianti Classico
- Tenuta di Arceno Chianti Classico Riserva

La Mozza I Perazzi Morellino di Scansano 2010—*I Love It*

85% Sangiovese, 5% Syrah, 5% Alicante, 2% Colorino, and 3% Ciliegiolo from Magliano, Tuscany, Italy. 13.5% Alcohol.

Suggested Retail Price: $16. Available for as low as $14.

From the winery:
> I Perazzi, the foundation of the La Mozza winery, was created to be unlike most typical Morellino di Scansano. The blend, which includes Mediterranean varieties, is more expressive and better demonstrates the potential of Maremma's terroir. I Perazzi is named after the pear-like fruit that grow on our estate and are depicted on the label.

This wine, a super Tuscan, is made primarily from Morellino di Scansano, which is the local name for Sangiovese. The super Tuscan designation is used for wines made in the Chianti zone that don't meet those stringent requirements. It allows producers to blend in other varieties not normally allowed in Chianti, which help give these wines a unique and excellent character. This example is priced quite low for a wine of this quality at just under $15.

The **2010 La Mozza I Perazzi Morellino di Scansano** begins with a wonderful aroma of licorice, spice, and black cherry. Tasting the wine reveals juicy red and black cherries, more licorice and spice, and soft and dusty tannins. This wine really needs some time to open up, but when it does it is fabulous. It ends dry with a bit of smoky tobacco and good length. This is simply a really delicious wine and it's just as good if not better on day two. Perfect with pizza, burgers, pasta, and other everyday fare.

Taste Rating: 9   **Cost Rating: 6**
Overall Rating: 8.3
Bulk Buy

MORE RECOMMENDED WINE FROM TUSCANY:
- Avignonesa Rosso di Montepulciano
- Bacci, Terre di Talamo "Tempo" Morellino di Scansano
- Capezzana Barco Reale di Carmignano
- Castello Banfi Rosso di Montalcino
- Il Poggione Rosso di Montalcino
- La Massa Toscana
- La Mozza I Perazzi Morellino di Scansano
- Mazzoni Rosso di Toscana
- Mantellassi Morellino di Scansano Riserva "Le Sentinelle"
- Poggio Argentiera Morellino di Scansano "Bellamarsilla"
- Poggio Nibbiale Morellino di Scansano
- Rosso di Altesino
- San Polo Rosso di Montalcino

Montefalco Rosso—*The Magic of Sagrantino*

Five Favorite Montefalco Rosso under $20

Montefalco Rosso? Sagrantino? Unfortunately these words don't mean much to the average wine drinker, but we're here to convince you why they should!

Montefalco is a special place in Umbria. Special for many reasons, but the one that concerns us is the Sagrantino grape. This grape is only grown in the Montefalco area and is unique in a lot of different ways. First off it has very low yields, which means it doesn't produce many grapes each harvest. The grapes it does produce ripen very late in the season and have extremely thick skins and accordingly extremely high polyphenols, which are the good antioxidants you read so much about in wine. In addition, Sagrantino has no known relationship to any other grape varieties in Italy. Lastly, it possesses the ability to make wines that age very gracefully, earning it the nickname "The Jewel of Umbria."

Of course being so unique also means that wines made from 100 percent Sagrantino (labeled as Sagrantino di Montefalco) come with a high price tag, way beyond our normal $20 limit. However, there is a way to sample this wonder grape without leaving our price range: **Montefalco Rosso.**

Montefalco Rosso wines are required to contain 60–70 percent Sangiovese, 10–15 percent Sagrantino, and 15–30 percent other varieties such as Merlot and Cabernet Sauvignon. You might be wondering (as we were) if only 10–15 percent Sagrantino can really make that much of a difference, but surprisingly it absolutely does. Unfortunately, even though there is about twice the amount of Montefalco Rosso produced as there is Montefalco Sagrantino, they can still be quite hard to find in the United States. There are a few reasons for this, the main one being that most of the wine never makes it out of Umbria, as it is consumed locally! In addition, in today's economy importers are reluctant to bring in new wines that consumers are unfamiliar with, which is a shame.

Luckily there are at least a few of these wines that have some form of distribution in the United States. Though they may still be hard to find, we encourage you to seek these out and experience the magic of Sagrantino!

First up is the 2009 Scacciadiavoli Montefalco Rosso.

A blend of 60% Sangiovese, 25% Merlot, and 15% Sagrantino from Montefalco, Umbria, Italy. 14% Alcohol.

Suggested Retail Price: $17. 4,600 cases produced. Imported by Selected Estates of Europe.

2009 Scacciadiavoli Montefalco Rosso.

From the winery:

Sangiovese, Sagrantino and Merlot grapes are hand-picked around the end of September and fermented at controlled temperature into stainless steel tanks. The wine ages in wooden barrels for 8 months prior to bottling and commercial release.

The **2009 Azienda Agraria Scacciadiavoli Montefalco Rosso** smells of black cherry, spice, cola, licorice, and dried herbs. These are some deep aromas; give your glass a good swirl to really enjoy them, and it gets even more expressive the more air it gets. Tasting reveals the perfect balance of tart dark fruit and oak along with a wonderful mouthfeel featuring soft yet grippy tannins. It ends dry with more luscious tart fruit that lingers for a long time.

Taste Rating: 10   Cost Rating: 4

Overall Rating: 8.5

Bulk Buy

Second is the 2010 Perticaia Montefalco Rosso.

A blend of 70% Sangiovese, 15% Colorino, and 15% Sagrantino from Montefalco, Umbria, Italy. 13.5% Alcohol.

Suggested Retail Price: $25. Available for as low as $15. 3,000 cases produced. Imported by Belvino, LLC.

From the winery:

Aging: Total of 18 months— as set by the wine producer's regulations. They are set as follows: 12 months in steel vats; 6 months in the bottle.

2010 Perticaia Montefalco Rosso.

Ideal With: This wine may be drunk throughout the meal. It goes especially well with salame and cold cuts, with pasta and first course dishes from the Umbrian cuisine and with Mediterranean cuisine in general.

Evolution: This is a wine that will evolve in the bottle so if it is stored properly it will mature for at least 5 years.

The **2010 Perticaia Montefalco Rosso** begins with a very pleasant bouquet of red fruits plus a little red licorice and even a whiff of perfumed floral notes. The wine is medium-bodied with lots of sour cherry, wild strawberry, and a little cranberry. This one is mostly fruit on day one but it's quite good and has a soft texture with mild tannins. It ends dry with medium-long length. It evolves even further on day two, where a really nice spice component develops.

Third is the 2009 Colle Ciocco Montefalco Rosso.

A blend of 70% Sangiovese, 15% Merlot, and 15% Sagrantino from Montefalco, Umbria, Italy. 14% Alcohol.

Suggested Retail Price: $16. 2,250 cases produced.

From the winery:

2009 Colle Ciocco Montefalco Rosso.

> Intense ruby-red colour. Deep and complex aroma, with flavours of plum, cherry and spices. It has good structure, is balanced and persistent, easy to drink. Ideal with strong-flavoured pasta dishes like strangozzi with truffle, tagliatelle with goose sauce and risotto with porcini mushrooms. Perfect with red meats main courses.

The **2009 Agricola Spacchetti Colle Ciocco Montefalco Rosso** begins with a very nice and quite complex aroma featuring plum, black cherry, a little black pepper, tobacco, and spice. The transformation on this wine with just a couple hours in the glass is tremendous—it's a fascinating wine to smell and taste every twenty to thirty minutes to watch it evolve. Tasting reveals spice, cola, a few oaky notes, and persistent sour cherry flavors all the way through the finish. It ends dry with slightly chewy tannins and good length.

Taste Rating: 9   Cost Rating: 5

Overall Rating: 8.0

Highly Recommended

Fourth is the 2010 Le Cimate Montefalco Rosso.

A blend of 60% Sangiovese, 15% Merlot, 15% Sagrantino, and 10% Cabernet Sauvignon from Montefalco, Umbria, Italy. 14.5% Alcohol.

Suggested Retail Price: $18.

From the winery:
Obtained from Sangiovese, Cabernet, Merlot and Sagrantino grapes. A clear, luminous and consistent colour. An inviting aroma, with hints of

2010 Le Cimate Montefalco Rosso.

plum and cherry. Warm, smooth and enveloping in the mouth, with an elegant tannin which perfectly blends the structure. Refined for 6 months after bottling, it combines perfectly with full flavoured first courses and grilled vegetables.

The **2010 Le Cimate Montefalco Rosso** begins with deep and enticing aromas of dark fruit, a little smoked meat, and a little mint. This is a very dry wine with a smooth and delicious texture and similar flavors to the nose when tasting. It's hard to believe this wine doesn't see any time in oak. It ends with a seriously lip-puckering dry finish with good length.

Taste Rating: 9   Cost Rating: 3

Overall Rating: 7.5

Recommended Buy

Last is the 2009 Romanelli Montefalco Rosso.

A blend of 65% Sangiovese, 15% Sagrantino, 10% Cabernet Sauvignon, and 10% Merlot from Montefalco, Umbria, Italy. 14.5% Alcohol.

Suggested Retail Price: $17. 1,250 cases produced.

From the winery:
> Aging: 12 months in French oak barrels of between 225 and 2,500 Litres. Minimum 6 months aging in bottle.

2009 Romanelli Montefalco Rosso.

> Aging Potential: 8-10 years
>
> Pairing Suggestion and Serving Temp: This wine can be enjoyed by itself or with food, such as red and white meats, charcuterie, or aged cheeses. Temperature 17C.

The **2009 Romanelli Montefalco Rosso** starts with wonderful aromas of dark berries, spice, and vanilla. Tasting reveals nice structure, lots of dark fruit, a bit of toasty oak, and dry, grippy tannins. This wine will stand up nicely to lots of different Italian dishes and is a great match with pizza. It ends dry with very good length and lingering dark berry and toasty oak notes.

Taste Rating: 9   **Cost Rating: 3**

Overall Rating: 7.5

Recommended Buy

MORE RECOMMENDED WINE FROM UMBRIA:
- Antonelli Montefalco Rosso
- Arnaldo Caprai Grecante Grechetto dei Colli Martani
- Arnaldo Caprai Montefalco Rosso
- Falesco Merlot
- Tenuta Castelbuono Montefalco Rosso
- Vitano Rosso

Masi Campofiorin Rosso Del Veronese 2009—*A Supervenetian That's Super Good*

70% Corvina, 25% Rondinella, and 5% Molinara from Verona, Veneto, Italy. 13.1% Alcohol.

Suggested Retail Price: $19. Available for as low as $13.

From the bottle:

Appaxximento countersigns Masi's expertise in the XXI century in the technique of obtaining greater concentra-

An original still going strong.

tion of aromas and tastes from grapes through the drying process.

Exclusive Masi 'Supervenetian' wine made since 1964 using red native grapes and produced with a technique developed by the Masi Technical Group.

Appearance: deep ruby red
Nose: ripe cherries and sweet spices
Palate: rich, powerful cherry and berry flavours, good length and soft tannins
Food pairing: versatile, excellent with pasta, risotto, grilled or roasted meat, and aged cheeses.

The **2009 Masi Agricola Campofiorin Rosso Del Veronese** is referred to as the original "Supervenetian" since it is one of the very first Valpolicella Ripasso wines. In the ripasso method, grapes are dried for many weeks after they are harvested, which allows the sugars to concentrate and become more powerful. These dried grapes are used to make excellent and expensive Amarone wines. In what can only be described as a stroke of genius, the leftover grape pomace (the remains of the grapes after being pressed—seeds, skins, stems, etc.) is effectively recycled by being refermented with standard Valpolicella wine. The goal is to add depth and complexity to a wine that is normally quite light-bodied.

This wine begins with a strong, beautiful aroma featuring black cherry, dried herbs, a little vanilla, and a hint of cinnamon. The wine tastes smooth and easy to drink with great flavor—primarily tart and juicy black cherry, cedar, raisin, and spice. It ends with good length, soft tannins, and more rich and savory fruit plus lingering tobacco notes. This is a really tasty wine that shows that the original is still going strong!

On a side note, we found this bottle to be a wonderful match for my wife's Pasta Fagiolo and, in fact, that pairing is what helped to bump my rating up to a Bulk Buy level. (It's also why we only publish reviews based on drinking wine normally, not from quick tastings.) I would expect it would work just as well with many other similar Italian dishes, so if you enjoy this style of food this is a great wine to keep on hand.

Taste Rating: 9   Cost Rating: 6
Overall Rating: 8.3
Bulk Buy

MORE RECOMMENDED WINE FROM VENETO:
- Allegrini Valpolicella
- Bolla Valpolicella
- Cantine Maschio Prosecco Brut
- Conte di Bregonzo Amarone Della Valpolicella
- Enza Prosecco
- Pasqua Ripasso Valpolicella Superiore
- Re Midas Corvina
- Valdo Nerello Mascalese Brut Rosé

Livio Felluga Vertigo 2009—*A Wine to Swoon Over*

75% Merlot and 25% Cabernet Sauvignon from Friuli-Venezia Giulia, Italy. 13% Alcohol.

Suggested Retail Price: $24. Available for as low as $17.

From the winery:
The blending of varietals in Vertigo serves two purposes. Merlot, which has been traditionally used in Friulan viticulture, forms a link between

Beautifully balanced and delicious. Plus I like the label.

Friuli and the rest of the world. Cabernet Sauvignon adds balance and complexity to the wine, giving Vertigo structure and aging potential.

Serving suggestions: Savoury pasta or rice dishes, grilled or stewed meat, beef, roast pork, lamb and goat, or moderately mature cheeses.

Despite the long-lasting stigma from the movie *Sideways*, some of us are big fans of Merlot. Merlot from Italy can be especially good. Although if I'm being completely honest, there's really only two reasons I originally decided to try this wine: 1) It's from Italy 2) I liked the label. While it's not a strategy I employ often, sometimes you get darn lucky . . .

The **2009 Livio Felluga Vertigo** begins with pleasant aromas of blackberry, plum, violets, strawberry, and a little anise. The wine tastes fantastic and features loads of jammy blackberry fruit, but this is far from a one-dimensional wine. You'll also find excellent spice plus secondary notes of cola and a little oak. To top it off all these delicious flavors are wrapped up in a silky smooth and lush texture. On the long, dry finish the spice comes to the forefront along with plenty more of that yummy juicy blackberry. Dizzyingly good!

Taste Rating: 9   **Cost Rating: 4**

Overall Rating: 7.8

Highly Recommended

MORE RECOMMENDED RED WINE FROM ITALY:
- Beni di Batasiolo Sovrena Barbera d'Alba
- Di Majo Norante Ramitello
- Fratelli Barba Colle Marino Montepulciano d'Abruzzo
- Leone de Castris Maiana Rosso Salice Salentino
- Luca Bosio Barbera d'Asti
- Mazzoni Piemonte Barbera
- Poderi Aldo Conterno Langhe Rosso
- Renato Ratti Barbera d'Alba
- Renato Ratti Barbera d'Asti
- Roscato Rosso Dolce
- Rubrato Aglianico dei Feudi di San Gregorio
- Stefano Farina Le Brume Langhe Rosso
- Tormaresca Neprica
- Saladini Pilastri Rosso Piceno
- Saladini Pilastri Pregio del Conte

Exploring the White Wines of Italy Including Two Bulk Buy Selections!

The words "Italian wine" no doubt conjure images of iconic wines like Barolo, Brunello, Chianti, and so forth, and rightly so. However, during the warm summer months the best thing coming out of Italy may well be the rich, mineral-soaked, delicious white wines made from all sorts of grapes you simply won't find anywhere else. In fact, Italy has more indigenous grapes than any other country in the world! Don't let the unknown names deter you—there is great delight to be had in all these indigenous varieties! Here are a couple of our very favorites.

First is the 2011 Nuraghe Crabioni Vermentino di Sardegna.

100% Vermentino from Sardinia. 13% Alcohol.

Suggested Retail Price: $21. Available for as low as $14.

From the winery:

Overlooking the Asinara Gulf, Nuraghe Crabioni is a 35 hectare property in the celebrated area of Sorso in Sassari, which is historically renowned for its viticulture. The vineyard benefits from its unique location, enjoying both warm southern winds and cooling maritime breezes. Nuraghe Crabioni wines flaunt a balanced, but distinct character.

Fantastic! Intriguing!

The **2011 Nuraghe Crabioni Vermentino di Sardegna** presents quite an intriguing aroma in the glass. You'll find lemon, almonds, dried herbs, sea salt, and mineral notes. Good acidity, good balance, salty and spicy mineral notes, and a rich and soft texture that is really pleasing to the mouth are just a few of the things you'll find. Tropical fruit and lemon carries into the finish where a touch of fennel also appears. Fantastic and intriguing, fantastically intriguing, or intriguingly fantastic—take your pick, just do yourself a favor and seek this one out!

Taste Rating: 9   Cost Rating: 6
Overall Rating: 8.3
Bulk Buy

Second is the 2011 Argillae Orvieto.

A blend of 60% Trebbiano and Grechetto 40% plus Chardonnay, Malvasi di Candia, and Sauvignon from Umbria, Italy. 13.5% Alcohol.

Suggested Retail Price: $17. Available for as low as $12.

From the bottle:
Orvieto is Umbria's—and one of Italy's—most famous white wines. Argillae Orvieto is dry, with a pleasant complexity of aromas, citrus, tropical fruits and floral scents. It pairs beautifully with hors d'oeuvres, salads, pasta with seafood or vegetables and light second courses.

So easy to drink and so delicous . . .

The **2011 Argillae Orvieto** begins with aromas of citrus, delicate floral notes, and a hint of tropical fruit. The wine tastes very fresh, rich, and flavorful in the mouth. This is another really tasty one, although don't drink it too cold to really enjoy it. There are even a few hints of nuts and a light spicy minerality that comes out on the excellent finish. Easy to drink and delicious!

Taste Rating: 9   **Cost Rating: 7**
Overall Rating: 8.5
Bulk Buy

MORE RECOMMENDED WHITE WINE FROM ITALY:
- Bastianich Friulano Adriatico
- Fontana Candida Frascati Superiore
- Mionetto Dolce Moscato
- OGIO Pinot Grigio
- Piccini Memoro Vino Bianco Italia
- Principessa Gavia Gavi
- Rocca Sveva Soave Classico
- Voveti Prosecco

Muros de Vinha Vinho Tinto 2010—*A Gem*

40% Tinta Roriz, 30% Touriga Franca, and 30% Tinta Barroca from Douro, Portugal. 13.5% Alcohol.

Suggested Retail Price: $12. Available for $6.99 at Costco.

From the bottle:
You have selected an exceptional and exclusive wine from an award winning winery. With a dense colour it shows aromas of cinnamon and jam. Has a perfect harmony with the fruit. Perfect for classic flavoured red meat dishes or cheese.

I noticed this wine at my local Costco several weeks before I finally bought a bottle and it continued to hang around in the store for quite a while after that. This leads me to believe it has been a slow seller, but don't let that scare you! Portugal has become so identified with fortified Port wines that its table (or non-fortified) wines are often criminally overlooked. (Fortified wines are called such because additional alcohol is added to them during fermentation, usually in the form of grape brandy.)

In fact, Portugal is so hot right now, you might even call it a reverse wine snob's dream. With an incredibly long history of quality winemaking and lots of established vineyards, there are a ton of inexpensive gems out there, just like this one.

The **2010 Quinta Do Portal Muros de Vinha Vinho Tinto** begins with pleasant aromas of red berry fruit and licorice along with hints of nutmeg and cinnamon. The wine tastes smooth with lots of spice and plenty of juicy fruit, although it's a bit darker in the mouth than the aromas of the bouquet suggest. There's also more licorice and nice acidity. It finishes dry with fine tannins and medium-long length. This one definitely drinks as though it costs way more than $7 and is a great example of the value to be found in Portugal.

Taste Rating: 8   **Cost Rating: 9**
Overall Rating: 8.3
Bulk Buy

Esporao Assobio Douro 2010—*Beautifully Done*

A blend of 40% Tinta Roriz, 40% Touriga Franca, and 20% Touriga Nacional from Douro, Portugal. 13.5% Alcohol.

Suggested Retail Price: $13. Available for as low as $10.

From the bottle:

> Assobio is the name of a hillside at Murcas Estate, where its highest vineyards are found. Each year we invite a photographer to portray the estate and its people. For the second Assobio harvest, we invited Jose Manuel Rodrigues. The photo was taken in October 2011.

We're big fans of the Douro region in Portugal. Wines made here typically consist of a blend of native Portuguese grapes that you've probably never heard of unless you're a Port drinker. Don't let that scare you away—if you're not trying wine from Portugal you're missing out. When wines like this one sell for only $10, you've just found the definition of extreme value.

The **2010 Esporao Quinta Dos Murcas Assobio Douro** begins with pleasant aromas of blackberry, black cherry, a little spice, and even a little raisin. Tasting the medium-bodied wine reveals great flavor, lovely spice, and lots of delicious fruit (red currant and black cherry primarily). You'll also find nice acidity and a great smooth, dry texture. Only 20 percent of the wine was aged in oak and for just six months. It ends with dry, tangy fruit flavors and lingering raisin/prune notes.

Taste Rating: 8　　　**Cost Rating: 8**

Overall Rating: 8.0

Highly Recommended

Quinta De La Rosa Douro Red 2009—*Perfection from Portugal (And It's Not Port)*

40% Touriga Nacional, 30% Touriga Franca, and 30% Tinta Roriz (Tempranillo) from the Douro, Portugal. 14.5% Alcohol.

Suggested Retail Price: $25. Available for as low as $16.

From the bottle:
Family owned and run, all Estate made from grape to bottle, 'A' graded grapes, low yields.

Grape Varieties: Touriga Nacional 40 percent, Tinta Roriz 30 percent and Touriga Franca 30 percent

Hand Picked. Matured in French barriques. Aged oak casks for 9 months.

Quinta de la Rosa was one of the pioneers in the endeavor to produce world-class table wines in the Douro region. While these nonfortified wines have been produced in the region for decades, it was just in the 1990s that they began to be taken more seriously and widely exported to the rest of the world.

The **2009 Quinta De La Rosa Douro Red** begins with a strong aroma of succulent ripe fruit that sucks you right in. The fabulous bouquet features blackberry, plum, and even a little banana, with vanilla and spice rounding it out. The wine tastes serious! This is a big and delicious full-bodied wine with wonderful complexity. The oak aging is done to perfection adding all the right notes without overdoing it. The La Rosa delivers a smooth, silky, and rich texture featuring concentrated, succulent fruit and layers of tasty spice. And despite the big and serious nature of this wine it is quite easy to drink. The finish goes on and on with sweet blackberry notes and loads of spice.

Taste Rating: 10   **Cost Rating: 5**

Overall Rating: 8.8

Bulk Buy

MORE RECOMMENDED RED WINE FROM PORTUGAL:
- Alente Red Trincadeira Aragonez
- Doural Tinto
- douRosa Douro Red Wine
- Dows Vale do Bomfim Douro Red
- Esporao 4 Quatro Castas
- J. Portugal Ramos Loios Vinho Tinto
- Montaria Red
- Quinta Do Portal Colheita Tinto
- Quinta Do Portal Reserva Red

Monte Velho White 2011—*A Summertime Slam Dunk*

35% Antao Vaz, 35% Roupeiro, and 30% Perrum from Alentejo, Portugal. 13.5% Alcohol.

Suggested Retail Price: $10. Available for as low as $8.

From the bottle:

From regional grape varieties, Roupeiro (35 percent), Antao Vaz (35 percent) and Perrum (30 percent), we produced this fresh and aromatic wine, with a well balanced fruity palate, and a clean acid finish.

When my thoughts begin to turn to warm weather and sun, I naturally think of pairing that warm weather with white wine on the patio. So even though it may be the dead of winter when you're reading this, it's never too early to begin planning for the dog days of summer. The **Esporao Monte Velho White** from Portugal is one you'll definitely want to consider for your patio-sipping enjoyment.

The wine begins with a fresh and fruity aroma of apple, pear, white peach, and a little citrus zest. Tasting the wine reveals one nice summertime sipper. It's fresh, fruity, and easy to drink with crisp acidity and a nice spicy mineral streak to add interest. It ends with lots of citrus-soaked mineral notes that last a surprisingly long time. A summertime slam dunk!

Taste Rating: 8   Cost Rating: 9
Overall Rating: 8.3
Bulk Buy

MORE RECOMMENDED WHITE WINE FROM PORTUGAL:
- Alvaro Castro DAC Dao Branco
- blue fin Vinho Verde
- Caves Vidigal Vinho Verde
- douRosa Douro White Wine
- Espiral Vinho Verde
- Jose Maria da Fonseca Twin Vines Vinho Verde
- Loios Vinho Branco
- Vera Vinho Verde

Stadlmann Gruner Veltliner 2011—*Gruner Love*

100% Gruner Veltliner from Thermenregion, Austria.
12.5% Alcohol.

Suggested Retail Price: $16.
Available for as low as $14.

From the bottle:
> Since 1780, the Stadlmann family has been producing wines made from the indigenous grapes of Austria's Thermenregion. Today, Johann Stadlmann VII continues this tradition, creating expressive and dynamic wines. "Gruner Veltliner," the most popular signature varietal of Austria, is a fresh yet well structured wine, with aromas of green apple and lime. This wine is perfect with fresh salads, seafood, poultry and light meat dishes.

Make your mouth come alive.

We've long been fans of Austrian wine, and although Austria produces tons of great wine, its claim to fame, pride and joy, national treasure, crown jewel, and magnum opus is Gruner Veltliner.

The variety is an offspring of the Traminer and St. Georgen grapes and makes up 29 percent of the vineyard acreage in Austria. Interestingly, St. Georgen was a previously unknown grape variety that was found as a single vine in an overgrown pasture that hadn't been used as a vineyard in over one hundred years. The link to Gruner was only able to be determined through DNA analysis. (Sounds like a new spin-off of CSI for wine lovers!)

Austria, with a latitude between Champagne and Burgundy, abundant mountains, and lots of rocky soils, is a prime area for growing grapes. The range of soil types and growing conditions also creates a fascinating study into just how different one grape can express itself. Gruner Veltliners I've tasted possessed a range of flavors from citrus to tropical to mineral to nutty to spicy. There was even one I noted as a "Dill Lover's Delight" due to its strong herbal flavors.

The **2011 Stadlmann Gruner Veltliner** begins with an enticing aroma of green apple, tropical fruit, and a little peach as well as white pepper and some mineral notes. The wine tastes bright, clean, and delicious with a fabulous, refreshing mouthfeel that simply makes your mouth come alive. You'll also find great acidity and tart fruit (green apple, pear, and lime) along with slightly salty minerals and a little white pepper and other spices. It ends with wonderful length—lime-soaked mineral notes linger in your mouth for a long time. One of the few white wines I've been tempted to buy by the case, this is truly an unforgettable wine.

Taste Rating: 9   **Cost Rating: 6**
Overall Rating: 8.3
Bulk Buy

MORE RECOMMENDED WHITE WINE FROM AUSTRIA:
- Austrian Pepper—Pfaffl 2011 Brut
- Charming Gruner Veltliner Reserve by Laurenz V.
- Domäne Wachau Terrassen Federspiel Grüner Veltliner
- Laurenz V. Singing Gruner Veltliner
- Obere Steigan-Huber 2011 Grüner Veltliner
- Schloss Gobelsburg Gobelsburger Gruner Veltliner
- Vom Schloss—Graf Hardegg Grüner Veltliner 2011

Zantho Zweigelt 2010—*A Perfect Wine for Thanksgiving Dinner!*

100% Zweigelt from Burgenland, Austria. 13% Alcohol.

Suggested Retail Price: $17. Available for as low as $12.

From the bottle:

Deep within the plains of the Seewinkel lies the village of Andau, which was first documented as Zantho in 1488. The region's gravelly soil, rich in minerals and iron, is ideal for producing high-quality red wines and for a rare genus of woodland lizard.

Josef Umathum and Wolfgang Peck make use of these optimum natural conditions to create wonderfully distinctive wines.

While most immediately think of Gruner Veltliner when they think of Austria, about one-third of the wine production in this region is actually red wine. And of that red wine, the most popular in the country is Zweigelt (Zvy-gelt). Not the best name for American consumers, I know, but don't let that stop you. Besides, Zweigelt is infinitely better than its original, and still occasionally used, name—Rotburger.

Zweigelt is a grape indigenous to Austria, and in fact, it was actually created in Austria in 1922 by Fritz Zweigelt. This was done by crossing two other indigenous grapes, St. Laurent and Blaufrankisch. Today Zweigelt accounts for about 14 percent of the total vineyard area in the country and about 40 percent of the red grape vineyard area. Today's selection comes from Burgenland, which is the easternmost region of Austria right next to Slovakia and Hungary and the area where much of the country's red wine is produced.

The **2010 Zantho Zweigelt** begins with spicy dark berry and cranberry aromas along with cinnamon and pepper. It needs a little time to breathe to really open up but then it is quite nice. A rather unique touch is that the bottle is sealed with a glass stopper rather than a cork. Tasting the wine reveals a creamy texture with flavors of smoky cranberry and other red berries, a little pepper, and more baking spice. The slightly dry finish features more of the same flavors. This is really quite a nice wine and a great introduction to Austrian reds.

One other note—my overwhelming thought when tasting this wine was that it would be perfect with many fall and winter meals, Thanksgiving dinner in particular, thanks to the cranberry and baking spice flavors. Just something to keep in mind as you do your wine shopping for all your holiday get-togethers, especially for your wine-loving friends and family that may not have tried this variety yet.

Taste Rating: 7   **Cost Rating: 7**

Overall Rating: 7.0

Recommended Buy

IBY Blaufrankisch Classic 2010—*A Beauty from Burgenland*

100% Blaufrankisch from Burgenland, Austria. 13% Alcohol.

Suggested Retail Price: $18. Available for as low as $16.

From the winemaker:

Radiant, very dark ruby garnet tones with hints of violet and a dark core. The violet color at the rim with the purple notes indicate the youth of the Blaufrankisch while the long legs in the glass reveal its high extract. Pronounced fruit of cherries and blackberries with pepper and spices. Dry in style with mild acidity and juicy tannins, and a long harmonious finish. A typical representative of local Blaufrankisch finished in the traditional style, it is fruity, spicy and inviting.

Blaufrankisch, which is indigenous to Austria, can also be found in places like Germany, Hungary, Bulgaria, the Czech Republic, and the United States. In Germany and the United States it is known as Lemberger most of the time. Here in the United States it is grown mainly in Washington State but you'll find small amounts in places like New York and Virginia. In Austria, Blaufrankisch is the second most grown red variety behind Zweigelt and is actually a parent to Zweigelt along with St. Laurent.

Blaufrankisch is a late ripening grape that is capable of producing wines with significant aging potential and prominent tannins. This is another example of a little-known variety excelling when it is grown in its native environment—there's a reason these varieties are indigenous to certain areas! Lucky for us, this one is priced right in our sweet spot, which is not always the case with lesser-known varieties.

The **2010 IBY Blaufrankisch Classic** begins with a really wonderful fruity aroma with tons of berry and a little baking spice. The wine also tastes very fruity with a plethora of berry flavors—mainly cranberry, red cherry, blueberry, and blackberry along with some pepper and spice. This is a lighter-bodied example of the variety and might even be good slightly chilled. It ends with more fruit and a nice medium-long finish. If you haven't tried Blaufrankisch I encourage you to; plus it's a perfect wine for the fall season!

Taste Rating: 8   **Cost Rating: 5**
Overall Rating: 7.3
Recommended Buy

Juris St. Laurent Selection 2010—*Pinot Noir's Deep, Dark, and Savory Love Child Finds a Home in Austria*

100% Saint Laurent from Neusiedlersee, Burgenland, Austria. 13% Alcohol.

Suggested Retail Price: $22. Available for as low as $16, but typically closer to $20.

From the winery:
> St. Laurent is a wild cross between Pinot Noir and an

unknown variety. Likely originating from France, it is now native to Burgenland. In the early 1980's, Axel's father Georg was among the first to focus on single varietal bottling of St. Laurent. The "Selection" St Laurent is sourced from vineyards of approximately 15 years cloned from the best of their old vines.

St. Laurent (aka Sankt Laurent or Saint Laurent) is the third major red grape grown in Austria. St. Laurent is believed to be the offspring of Pinot Noir and another, unknown red grape. It is also one of the parents of Zweigelt along with Blaufrankisch. Those two varieties make up the remaining major Austrian red grape varieties we've already covered.

The **2010 Juris St. Laurent Selection** begins with deep and dark aromas of black pepper, dark fruit, leather, spice, and violet. Together all these components create a very enticing, earthy aroma that reminds me of a Cabernet Franc. When tasting the wine the deep and dark theme continues with really tasty sour dark fruit, more black pepper and earthy notes, and a little leather. Add in nice grippy tannins, good acidity, and a substantial smooth mouthfeel and you have a really savory wine. It ends with succulent dark fruit, a bit on the sour side, and good length. Another awesome Austrian!

Taste Rating: 9   **Cost Rating: 5**

Overall Rating: 8.0

Highly Recommended

MORE RECOMMENDED RED WINE FROM AUSTRIA:
- Juris Pinot Noir Selection
- Juris Zweigelt
- Meinhard Forstreiter Zvy-Gelt Zweigelt
- Weingut Gernot and Heike Heinrich Red
- Weingut J. Heinrich Blaufrankisch
- Weingut Moric Blaufrankisch

A Hidden Gem—Slovenia's Remarkable and Affordable Wine

A rich and historic wine culture combines with modern winemaking techniques to create what could be the next big thing in white wine.

Slovenia, part of the former Yugoslavia, represents a fascinating mix of traditional (old) and modern (new) that somehow manages to balance that line extremely well. Slovenia borders Italy on the west, Croatia on the east, Austria to the north, and just a bit of Hungary to the northeast. The entire country is the size of New Jersey, half of which is forest. Two million people live here. They speak Slovenian but most also speak English as well as Italian, Croatian, or German.

Despite the country's small size, it has an almost stunning array of terrains. From the 45 km of coastline on the Adriatic Sea right next to Italy it takes less than three hours to get to the Austrian Alps.

Grapes have been grown here throughout history, and taking a look at its location next to Italy and under Austria, it's easy to see why. This long history of winemaking hit a bit of a bump in the

The Adriatic Sea in Koper, Slovenia.

road after WWII when Yugoslavia came under socialist rule. Vineyards (and other businesses) were nationalized, which meant ownership was transferred to the government who then decided what grapes could be grown and how much of each wine could be made.

Yet the wine industry endured and produced incredible stories like that of the Conrad Furst family members who first established their vineyard in Slovenia in 1821. In 1945 their vineyard, like all the rest in the country, was nationalized. In addition because they were of German descent they were exiled from the country.

This, however, was not the end of the story. When Slovenia gained its independence in 1992 and the country began the process of denationalization, the family was able to apply to get its vineyard back. Thirteen years later, after proving they were not "political" (the code word for Nazis), they regained their vineyard. The only problem was that the grandfather was the last one to make wine in the family and he was now in his nineties! The rest of the family had moved on to other successful careers, but they are now relearning how to manage a vineyard and make wine.

The wines of Conrad Furst & Sohne.

We also heard stories of families (through unnamed methods) growing nonapproved grapes during this period of government control, or holding back more wine than they were allowed. In fact, one of the more amazing moments of our trip was exploring the cellar full of vintage wines at p&f wineries. The winery is situated in what is considered the best wine growing region in the country, Podravje, which is just under Austria and next to Croatia. Its specialty is white wine.

It was here that my whole conception of how white wines can age was turned upside down.

In examining the archive cellar, a 1959 Riesling is not unexpected—after all Riesling is certainly one white grape that can age quite gracefully. But a 1963 Sauvignon Blanc that is the pride of the cellar? We tasted a 1971 Pinot Blanc (late harvest) that was fresher and fruitier than many 2012 wines on the market. This cellar was full of amazing finds, and in fact, they even have a website dedicated to it.

This tiny country is full of treasures like this. The food was absolutely fantastic, with one of the most memorable meals happening at Restaurant Bric in Koper.

Tasting the 1971 Late Harvest Pinot Blanc.

Here we sampled the local specialty of sea bass baked in a salt crust, which was so good I believe I ate it at least once every day on the trip. An even bigger treat at Restaurant Bric were the truffles. We even met the owner of the restaurant who hunts for the truffles himself with several of his truffle dogs. The pictures below attest to their proficiency at finding these treasures!

Our tour of Slovenia began here in the Koper region, which is by the Adriatic Sea and is absolutely gorgeous. We visited the Vinakoper winery (which is the second largest in Slovenia) along with several other winemakers from the area.

Although white wine is made throughout the country, the Koper region is one of the better areas for red grapes. Refosk, which is made into a full-bodied sparkling red unlike anything I've ever tried, was a special treat. (Refosk is also referred to as Terran locally.) Malvasia is also indigenous to this area. A few of the vineyards in this area even cross over the Italian border with a fence running down the middle.

Salt-Baked Sea Bass at Restaurant Bric in Koper, Slovenia.

From there we went to the country's oldest city, Ptuj (you pronounce it like ptooey), which is on the other side of the country, near Austria (and the Alps) and Croatia. There is a fantastic wine trail, called the Jeruzalem Wine Road, going around the mountains in this area that gives you the opportunity to visit a number of wineries. The name comes from Jews who were reportedly on their way to the Holy Land in Israel. They liked the area (and the wine) so much that they stayed instead of continuing their journey!

The idyllic city of Ptuj.

This area is also where p&f wineries is located, which is itself an amazing juxtaposition of old winemaking techniques and traditions combined with some of the most technologically advanced systems I've ever seen.

There's the original five-story gravity flow building contrasted with the new inert gas system that takes oxygen down to 2 percent (from a normal of 21 percent) after grapes are sorted and destemmed. This not only helps to maintain the freshness of the grapes and reduce oxidation but also allows the use of less sulfur because microorganisms can't grow.

Despite this high technology, all grapes are still handpicked, yet grapes only go two hours from picking to press. There are also the fully computerized stainless steel tanks that range in size from 1,500 to 240,000 liters so that any size block of grapes can be fermented together.

The stated goal in all of this is to maintain the fresh and fruity character of the grapes all the way into the bottle. Based on the many wines we tasted from both the puklavec & friends and the Gomila brands, it appears that p&f wineries has succeeded mightily in this regard.

Particular favorites were the Pinot Grigio/Sauvignon Blanc blend, which I think is tailor-made for the U.S. market, several wines made from the local variety of Furmint (the same variety used to make Hungarian Tokaji wines), and a unique and delicious sparkling Sauvignon Blanc that managed to retain the typical Sauvignon Blanc characteristics in a sparkling wine.

I am extremely excited for these wines to gain distribution here in the United States, which is just starting. The best news is that they will be available for well under $20.

Shiny new tanks.

Our trip ended in the capital and largest city of Slovenia, Ljubljana. From the incredible open-air market to the famous statue called the Ljubljana dragon, the city is full of history. It's also just about the perfect size—big enough that there is plenty to do and see but not so big that you get lost or overwhelmed. It reminded me a bit of Copenhagen with the river running right through the middle of the city. If you go be sure to check out the main square in the old town area, which has a statue of France Prešeren, a famous nineteenth-century Slovene poet who wrote the country's national anthem.

The Ljubljanica River flows through the center of Ljubljana.

You know this is a country full of winelovers when the national anthem is literally a toast!

All in all, this was an eye-opening experience into this hidden gem of a country.

puklavec & friends Sauvignon Blanc & Pinot Grigio 2012—*Highly Quaffable*

70% Sauvignon Blanc and 30% Pinot Grigio from Stajerska, Slovenia. 12.5% Alcohol.

Suggested Retail Price: $15. Available for around $12.

From the bottle:
In the hills around the village of Jerusalem in Eastern Slovenia lies a unique, small winegrowing region. Here, all our grapes are still handpicked to create an interesting blend of Sauvignon Blanc and Pinot Grigio. A fruity, accessible wine with aromas of passion fruit and lemon underscored by a surprising pepperiness. A long, fresh, aftertaste that goes very well with meat dishes, salads and especially asparagus.

The wines of Slovenia are on the rise.

The **2012 puklavec & friends Sauvignon Blanc & Pinot Grigio** begins with pretty typical Sauvignon Blanc aromas of lemongrass, tropical fruit, and citrus but it's in the taste that the Pinot Grigio makes its presence known. The wine is wonderfully drinkable, combining the best of both varieties with the Pinot Grigio adding a level of fruitiness. Frankly I'm surprised we don't see this blend more often. The best part, however, is the wonderful finish that features lingering lemon and guava spiked with a fantastic spicy pepper streak.

Taste Rating: 9   **Cost Rating: 7**

Overall Rating: 8.5

Bulk Buy

SOUTH AMERICA

Wine has been made all over South America for hundreds of years but it is still considered a relatively new region to the wine scene. Wines from Argentina and Chile get most of the headlines but there is also a lot of quality wine being made in places like Brazil and Uruguay.

Argentina—Argentina has long been associated with Malbec; a lot of them are great and cost under $20. However, with more and more producers jumping on the bandwagon, the overall quality of Malbec from Argentina has taken a bit of a dip. Luckily Malbec isn't the only variety that thrives in Argentina. One of my favorites is the highly aromatic white variety of Torrontés.

Chile—Chile is a stunning country. It's 2,700 miles long of ocean and mountain. This varied terroir is a winemaker's dream and the country has burst onto the wine scene in the last few years, first with Carmenere, the red variety most associated with the country, but as of late with just about every other variety as well. It's an exciting time to explore all this country has to offer.

Uruguay—If you like big, dark, tannic wines, Uruguay is one country you definitely want to keep on your radar. In the last five to ten years winemakers there have concentrated on what they are calling their signature grape: Tannat. These wines will still be a bit hard to find for now, but snatch them up if you see them. Tannat is to Uruguay what Malbec is to Argentina. Since this region is just starting to gain recognition there is great value to be found.

Dona Paula Estate Black Edition Red Blend 2012—
Much More Than Malbec

60% Malbec, 37% Cabernet Sauvignon, and 3% Petit Verdot from Lujan de Cuyo, Mendoza, Argentina. 14.1% Alcohol.

Suggested Retail Price: $15. Available for as low as $13.

From the bottle:
Inspired by the varietals that grow best in Lujan de Cuyo, our winemaker crafted this blend of Malbec, Cabernet Sauvignon and Petit Verdot.

A delightful dry Bordeaux blend from Mendoza.

A rich purple in color, this wine has aromas of plum, spices and red pepper with delicate notes of mint. Velvety tannins, a good body and a long, persistent finish balance this wine nicely.

Try this wine with red meats such as beef tenderloin medallions. Our vineyards are managed using sustainable agricultural practices.

Argentina is known for its excellent Malbec, but that's not the only wine it produces. There's plenty of good wine (at very good prices) coming out of Argentina that is not Malbec; however, if you're not feeling that adventurous we've got a good compromise for you—an excellent red blend containing 60 percent Malbec.

The **2012 Dona Paula Estate Black Edition Red Blend** begins with pleasant aromas of plum, black cherry, mint, a little vanilla, and, as the label says, a touch of red pepper. Tasting reveals a delightful dry Bordeaux blend with lots of dark fruit, spice, and vanilla. Nicely balanced with good acidity and a delicious smooth texture, this wine doesn't scream Malbec and that's OK. It ends dry with very tart fruit, more spice, and good length. Pair it with a steak or other grilled meats and you'll be very happy.

Taste Rating: 9   **Cost Rating: 6**

Overall Rating: 8.3

Bulk Buy

RECOMMENDED RED WINE FROM ARGENTINA:
- Anoro Malbec
- BenMarco Cabernet Sauvignon
- BenMarco Malbec
- Bodega Amalaya
- Bodegas Caro Amancaya Gran Reserva
- Bodega Amalaya
- Bodega Monteviejo Lindaf lor Petite F leur
- Bodega Norton Malbec Reserva
- Bodega Sottano Classico Cabernet Sauvignon
- Coquena Tannat
- Graffigna Centenario Reserve Malbec

Hermanos Malbec Tannat 2011—*Malbec with a Deep, Dark, and Delicious Twist*

70% Malbec and 30% Tannat from Valle de Cafayate, Salta, Argentina. 13.9% Alcohol.

Suggested Retail Price: $15. Available for as low as $13.

From the bottle:

Brothers—we played soccer, we fought a lot, we generally caused trouble for our parents. But we Domingo Brothers ("Hermanos" in Spanish)

A standout in a sea of Malbec.

became the best of friends, and 50 years after our father and uncle opened a winery, we started one of our own on a hillside above Cafayate. We named the winery Domingo Molina—Domingo for our father's last name and Molina for our mother's. Over the decades, our family has located the best vineyard sites in Salta Province, all 5,800–7,300 feet above sea level. This extreme altitude and 340 days of sun yield wines with intense aromas and soft tannins which are a pleasure to drink, especially with our brothers—Osvaldo, Gabriel & Rafael—the Hermanos de Domingo Molina.

Tannat (pronounced Ta-Not) has taken on a new life in South America. Originally grown primarily in southwest France, it has now become quite common in Uruguay, Brazil, Peru, Bolivia, and Argentina. This is an up-and-coming varietal that produces seriously big, tannic wines. Some even feel that Tannat could be Uruguay's Malbec—the variety that puts it on the wine map like Malbec did for Argentina. This wine clocks in at only 30 percent Tannat, but even that amount is sufficient to help this wine stand out from the crowd.

The first thing you notice about the **2011 Domingo Molina Hermanos Malbec-Tannat** is how dark and inky it is in the glass, no doubt thanks to the Tannat. The wine begins with strong, dense aromas of blackberries, plums, olives, and mint dark chocolate (any wine that smells of mint dark chocolate is certainly a friend of mine.) Tasting the wine reveals wonderful dark fruit with the Tannat adding a bigness to the wine that separates it from your average Malbec. The flavors when tasting are similar to the bouquet just wrapped up in a really silky, velvety texture. You'll also find some nice mineral notes. It ends dry, with dusty tannins and good length. A deep, dark, and delicious twist on your standard Malbec!

Taste Rating: 9   **Cost Rating: 6**
Overall Rating: 8.3
Bulk Buy

MORE RECOMMENDED RED WINE FROM ARGENTINA:
- Kaiken Terroir Series Corte Malbec Blend
- Kaiken Ultra Malbec
- Luca Laborde Double Select Syrah
- Santa Julia Innovacion Bonarda-Cabernet Sauvignon
- Santa Julia [+] Malbec
- Trapiche Broquel Malbec
- Trivento Amado Sur Malbec
- Trivento Reserve Malbec
- Zolo Bonarda
- Zuccardi Q Tempranillo

La Reina Torrontés 2013— *Summertime Sipping at Its Best*

Torrontés from Mendoza, Argentina. 13% Alcohol.

Suggested Retail Price: $13. Available at that price.

From Argentina with love.

From the winery:
Torrontés is the hottest thing to arrive from Argentina since the tango. Not to be confused with Spain's Torrontés (that's a completely different fruit), the Argentine queen is a leader of the pack. She's highly aromatic, exuberantly floral, with a rich, hothouse citrus scent—a whiff will have you wondering whether La Reina should be sold as a wine or a perfume. But one sip will have you lining up for another pour of her tropical peach, apricot, and kiwi flavors that come with a crisp, zingy pop. Queue your clique because this ringleader knows how to rock a party.

As much as we love a good Mendoza Malbec, Torrontés may be the best thing coming out of Argentina these days. It's perfect for both warmer days and colder winters when you're stuck inside, dreaming about warm days on the patio sipping this highly aromatic and refreshing variety.

The **2013 La Reina ("The Queen") Torrontés** begins with a pleasant, aromatic bouquet of flowers, citrus, tropical fruit, and even a whiff of a nutty note. Tasting the wine reveals similar flavors to the nose, but they go deep. There's also some really nice spice, adding complexity and a wonderful racy acidity and mouthfeel. It ends dry with a little spicy minerality under the delicious fruit and features really good length.

Taste Rating: 9   **Cost Rating: 6**

Overall Rating: 8.3

Bulk Buy

MORE RECOMMENDED WHITE WINE FROM ARGENTINA:
- Bandana Chardonnay-Torrontés
- Bodegas Callia Alta Torrontés
- Bodega Colomé Torrontés
- Crios Torrontés
- Elsa Bianchi Torrontés

New Age White Wine—*The Definition of Refreshing*

A nonvintage, semisparkling blend of 90% Torrontés and 10% Sauvignon Blanc from Mendoza, Argentina. 9% Alcohol.

Suggested Retail Price: $10. Available for as low as $8.

From the bottle:
Argentina's most popular white wine is a refreshing blend of 10 percent Sauvignon Blanc and 90 percent Torrontés. The intense fruit and floral aromas lead to a soft, sensual wine. New Age should be enjoyed chilled by itself or as a "Tincho." The "Tincho," one of the most popular cocktails in Argentina, is created by pouring New Age over ice and garnishing with a lime wedge. Cheers!

The **New Age White** is a certified summertime sipper if there ever was one! When the temperature really heats up I can't think of many wines that would be more refreshing than this bubbly little number from Valentin Bianchi. It begins with a pleasant, peachy aroma that also features a little tropical fruit. Tasting the wine reveals sweet yet crisp flavors of peach, pear, and mango and a really nice effervescence that cuts down the sweetness nicely. You'll also find good acidity in this very refreshing wine. And I love the low alcohol so you don't have to be too concerned if you're quaffing it down on a really hot day. As the label says you can even serve it over ice with a lime, called the Tincho in Argentina. There's good reason this was the top selling Argentine white wine in the United States in 2010!

Taste Rating: 8　　　**Cost Rating: 9**

Overall Rating: 8.3

Bulk Buy

MORE RECOMMENDED WHITE WINE FROM ARGENTINA:
- Famiglia Meschini Sparkling Torrontés
- Familia Zuccardi Santa Julia[+] Torrontés
- Recuerdo Wines Torrontés
- Trivento Reserve Torrontés
- Trumpeter Torrontés

Casa Silva Los Lingues Gran Reserva Carménère 2008—
Tour of Chile

100% Carménère from Colchagua Valley, Chile. 14% Alcohol.

Suggested Retail Price: $22. Available for as low as $16.

From the bottle:
> This Carmenere is from the Los Lingues Estate tucked away in the Northeastern corner of Colchagua Valley, in the foothills of the magnificent Andes Mountains. Among many other awards as Chile's top Carmenere producer, Casa Silva recently won the trophy at the Wines of Chile Awards as the Best Chilean Carmenere. This wine, of superlative colour, has great concentration of silky elegant tannins, hints of chocolate and a very long finish.

Chile is an incredible country both in terms of geography—it is 2,700 miles long but no more than 100 miles wide—and in terms of winemaking, with a rich history dating back to the 1500s. Nowadays, thanks to a fortuitous turns of events, the signature grape of the country is Carménère.

Originally from France, this grape in the Cabernet family was brought over from the Bordeaux in the nineteenth century because it was believed to be Merlot. The grape thrived in Chile but it wasn't until 1998 that it was officially recognized as the distinct variety of Carménère. And as it turns out the grape is rarely planted in France today.

The **2008 Casa Silva Los Lingues Gran Reserva Carménère** begins with aromas of ripe dark fruit and green pepper. The wine tastes of lots of blackberry and blueberry flavors but also spice, oak, and herb notes. This wine has lots of sweet fruit but it doesn't overwhelm. The Casa Silva finishes with a good amount of oak and a little lingering tobacco. Not too bad on day one, but this wine was really delicious on day two as the oak was toned way down. In fact, I liked it so much better that I even revised my Taste rating up from a 7 to an 8, so be sure to give this one some air before drinking.

Taste Rating: 8   **Cost Rating: 5**

Overall Rating: 7.3

Recommended Buy

MORE RECOMMENDED RED WINE FROM CHILE:
- Casillero del Diablo Reserva Winemaker's Red Blend
- Concha y Toro Gran Reserva Serie Riberas Carménère
- Concha y Toro Gran Reserva Serie Riberas Malbec
- Concha y Toro Marques de Casa Concha Carménère
- Cousino-Macul Finis Terrae
- De Martino Legado Reserva Cabernet Sauvignon-Malbec
- Emiliana Natura Merlot
- Haras de Pirque Character Cabernet Sauvignon/Carménère
- Koyle Reserva Cabernet Sauvignon
- Maquis Cabernet Sauvignon
- Merino Syrah
- Montes Twins Red Wine
- Montgras Quatro
- Santa Carolina Reserva de Familia Carménère
- Santa Rita Medalla Real Gran Reserva Carménère
- Toro de Piedra Syrah-Cabernet Sauvignon Reserva

Mayu Pedro Ximenez 2012—*A Great Wine from a Grape You've Never Heard Of*

100% Pedro Ximenez from Elqui Valley, Chile. 12.5% Alcohol.

Suggested Retail Price: $15. Available for as low as $12.

From the bottle:
In the northern edge of Chile lies the Elqui Valley, a place of bright days and cold nights. It's perfect for growing grapes and gazing at what the Incas called Mayu—the river of stars in the Milky Way. For this reason, you will see eight observatories here, all studying the heavens.

Meet Pedro Ximenez: A grape varietal long used in the production of brandy and sherry makes a surprisingly delicious wine.

A stylish white wine, with appealing aromas of lemon and lime, balanced by fresh acidity. Long finish and mineral character makes this an excellent match for shellfish and seafood.

The Elqui Valley is one of the newest regions for producing wine in Chile. In fact, Vina Mayu, which was started in 2005, was the first winery in the valley. The Elqui Valley has long been known for producing the best grapes for Pisco. Pisco is a type of grape brandy made in Peru and Chile. One of the primary grapes they use is Pedro Ximenez. (This variety is also planted in Spain where it is used in sherry.)

Pedro Ximenez is generally considered unsuitable for table wines due to a lack of acidity. Whether that is overcome by the unique conditions of the Elqui Valley, the age of vines, or something else altogether I don't know, but I do know that there was no evidence of a lack of acidity in this wine.

The **2012 Vina Mayu Pedro Ximenez** begins with pleasant aromas of citrus, lime, and a streak of almost fresh-smelling minerals (if it's possible for minerals to smell fresh). The wine tastes really delicious with similar flavors to the nose and features a fresh, bright, and lively mouthfeel with some nice underlying minerality. It ends crisp and tasty with the citrus turning tart and that fresh minerality continuing—a refreshing wine that is just a delight to drink!

Taste Rating: 8   Cost Rating: 7
Overall Rating: 7.8
Highly Recommended

MORE RECOMMENDED WHITE WINE FROM CHILE:
- Concha Y Toro Marques De Casa Concha Chardonnay
- Cono Sur Bicicleta Riesling
- Cono Sur Vision Single Vineyard Loma Roja Sauvignon Blanc
- De Martino Legado Reserva Chardonnay
- Los Vascos Barons de Rothschild (Lafite) Sauvignon Blanc
- Santa Rita Medalla Real Gran Reserva Chardonnay
- TerraNoble Sauvignon Blanc
- Veramonte Ritual Sauvignon Blanc
- Vina Casablanca Nimbus Single Vineyard Sauvignon Blanc
- Vina Tabali Reserva Viognier

Artesana Tannat 2011—*A Breakthrough*

100% Tannat from Canelones, Uruguay. 15% Alcohol.

Suggested Retail Price: $20. Available for as low as $17.

From the bottle:
Artesana is an ultra-premium boutique winery located in the acclaimed Canelones region of Uruguay. Tannat (originally from France) is the signature varietal of Uruguay and produces balanced, full-bodied wines with ripe fruit flavors and an exotic, spicy character.

Artesana's unique artisan wines are made from 100 percent estate-grown grapes and handcrafted by our two exceptional women winemakers. Wines are made in small lots fermented separately, aged for 12 months in the highest quality French and American oak, custom blended, and bottled without fining or filtration. Smooth and well-rounded, the rich palate of this Tannat bottling delivers a complex layering of ripe blackberry, dark chocolate, smoky oak and spice, seamlessly nuanced in a long, generous finish.

In a story that parallels the rise of Malbec in Argentina, Tannat is a grape variety that although originally from France is little used there today except as a blend component. It has, however, found new life in South America, much like Malbec did, and specifically in Uruguay. And while you probably haven't heard much about Tannat or wine from Uruguay, that is likely about to change.

The **2011 Artesana Tannat** begins with a pleasant aroma featuring dark fruit, dark chocolate, floral notes, and dried herbs. The wine tastes like the name seems to suggest—quite tannic—

but I like it. There's more dark fruit and dark chocolate plus a little licorice and some savory herbs. Tarry, black tea notes come to the front on the long, dry finish along with a taste of raisin underneath. Quite nice for lovers of big, tannin-driven wines.

Taste Rating: 8   **Cost Rating: 4**

Overall Rating: 7.0

Recommended Buy

MORE RECOMMENDED WINE FROM URUGUAY:
- Artesana Tannat-Merlot
- Bouza Tannat
- Pisano Rio de Los Pajaros Reserve Tannat
- Pueblo del Sol Reserva Tannat
- Pueblo del Sol Tannat

AUSTRALIA/NEW ZEALAND

Australian Shiraz and New Zealand Sauvignon Blanc, what else is there to know, right? Well, not quite. Both countries offer a whole lot more than that. Do you like Pinot Noir, but don't like paying Oregon or California prices? Check out New Zealand. Want a wine you can serve with brunch instead of a mimosa? Check out our fresh and fizzy pick from Australia.

Red Knot Shiraz 2012 by Shingleback—*Bring On the Barbecue*

92% Shiraz and 8% Grenache from McLaren Vale, Australia. 14% Alcohol.

Suggested Retail Price: $18. Available for as low as $12.

From the bottle:
Red Knot: a rich wine from the McLaren Vale region of South Australia. Known for its beautiful scenery, Mediterranean climate and award winning wines, McLaren Vale vineyards produces grapes that are rich in flavour and filled with distinctive characteristics.

Juicy, spicy, and tasty Shiraz.

Vibrant in colour and highly aromatic, this intensely varietal Shiraz displays ripe strawberry and blackberry fruit and is subtly framed with American and French oak.

The first thing that stands out about this wine is not the wine itself or even the label but the unusual closure called a zork.

The Zork is popular with home winemakers and it's also the first resealable closure for sparkling wines. Opening is as simple as tearing off the spiral strip and then popping the plastic cork (which you can later use to reseal the bottle). In keeping with our stance against wine snobbery, the Zork is just fine with us.

The **2012 Red Knot Shiraz by Shingleback** smells jammy with lots of black cherry and plum aromas but you'll also find secondary notes of licorice, vanilla, and just a hint of dark chocolate. Tasting also reveals lots of jammy fruit in this medium-bodied wine as well as some really nice spice, good acidity, and fine tannins that make this easy and fun to drink. It ends with even more jammy fruit along with some oaky notes. That hint of dark chocolate from the nose also returns to wrap things up nicely. This one will make a great match with barbecue!

Taste Rating: 8   **Cost Rating: 7**

Overall Rating: 7.8

Highly Recommended

MORE RECOMMENDED RED WINE FROM AUSTRALIA:
- Chateau Tanunda Grand Barossa Shiraz
- d'Arenberg The Stump Jump Red
- George Wyndham Founder's Reserve Shiraz
- Hardys Nottage Hill Shiraz
- Jacob's Creek Reserve Coonawarra Cabernet Sauvignon
- Leeuwin Estate Siblings Margaret River Shiraz
- McWilliam's Hanwood Estate Shiraz
- Penley Estate Gryphon Coonawarra Merlot
- Peter Lehmann Clancy's
- Redbank Fighting Flat King Valley Shiraz
- Robert Oatley Margaret River Cabernet Sauvignon
- Shoofly Shiraz
- Wyndham Estate Bin 555 Shiraz
- Yalumba Eden Valley Shiraz Viognier
- Zonte's Footstep Lake Doctor Shiraz

Innocent Bystander Pink Moscato 2011—*A Beauty for Breakfast*

A blend of Gordo Muscat and Black Muscat from Yarra Valley, Victoria, Australia. 5.5% Alcohol.

Suggested Reatil Price: $14. Available widely for around $10 for the 750ml bottle. Also available in 375ml bottles.

From the winery:
  Tastes like kisses and if it were any fresher you'd slap it!

A delightfully fresh and fizzy pick.

Nose: Sticky real Turkish Delight. Fruit tingle, sherbet, fairy floss, fresh fuzzy peach.
Palate: Raspberry jelly, peach sherbet, rosewater. Clean and crisp.
Food: Fresh pancakes with poached fruit, cheese plate with muscadels, on its own as an apertif.

It's not often you can recommend a wine for breakfast, but that is exactly what we have with this wine. After all, why should mimosas have all the fun? At only 5.5 percent alcohol today's selection will play the part perfectly, and with its natural effervescence and good acidity it's a great match for all kinds of breakfast and brunch foods! On top of all that the crown seal closure on the bottle (aka a bottle cap) makes for a distinctive look at your brunch table.

The **2011 Innocent Bystander Pink Moscato** begins with pleasant aromas of strawberry, peach, watermelon, roses, and ginger ale. The wine tastes delightfully fun with fresh and fizzy flavors of red berries, peach, strawberry, and zesty citrus. Moderately sweet, but nowhere near cloying, and with just the right amount of bubbles, this wine is sure to please. It ends with more sweet fruit notes that linger a long time. Serve it up at your next brunch and let the compliments flow!

Taste Rating: 8   **Cost Rating: 8**

Overall Rating: 8.0

Highly Recommended

MORE RECOMMENDED WHITE AND ROSÉ WINE FROM AUSTRALIA:
- Angove Zibibbo Sparkling Pink Moscato
- d'Arenberg The Stump Jump White
- FishEye Riesling
- Frisk Prickly Riesling
- Jacob's Creek Reserve Barossa Dry Riesling
- Matthew Iaconis Margaret River Sauvignon Blanc + Semillon
- Peter Lehmann Layers Adelaide White
- Plantagenet Omrah Unoaked Chardonnay
- The Lucky Country Rosé
- Zonte's Footstep Doctoress di Lago Pinot Grigio

Mt. Beautiful North Canterbury Pinot Noir 2011—*Brings Its A-Game*

Pinot Noir from Cheviot Hills, North Canterbury, South Island, New Zealand. 14% Alcohol.

Suggested Retail Price: $24 and available for as low as $18. 2,650 cases produced.

From the bottle:
> Inspired by a bold vision from David and Leigh Teece, the picturesque Mt Beautiful vineyard is located in an intriguing new wine region—Cheviot Hills, North Canterbury, in the South Island of New Zealand.
>
> Sheltered from the cool ocean breezes by the nearby Mt Beautiful, the vines grace north-facing slopes of coastal foothills. Here, the warm, dry climate and alluvial silt loam soils are ideal for growing the highest quality grapes.

I love it when a wine comes together.

Being a child of the 1980s, *The A-Team* was a Tuesday night staple in our household. And if you're familiar with the show you know that during every episode there inevitably comes a point (no matter how impossible it may have seemed) when all their crazy plans somehow succeed and Hannibal sticks a cigar in his mouth and utters his famous phrase, "I love it when a plan comes together." That's exactly what popped into my mind when tasting this wine.

The **2011 Mt. Beautiful North Canterbury Pinot Noir** begins with a lovely nose of cranberry, black cherry, a little oak, a little baking spice, and some nice floral notes. It's a bit subdued at first but actually quite complex, and I enjoyed it very much. The wine tastes silky smooth with lots of tart black cherry, strawberry, and cranberry plus some really lovely spice. Medium-bodied, with good acidity, the wine has absolutely fabulous balance—it's one of those wines where everything just comes together. It ends fantastically, with a long, cranberry- and spice-tinged finish.

If you think great Pinot Noir has to come from Oregon, France, or California, think again—I pity the fool who doesn't appreciate this Pinot Noir from New Zealand!

Taste Rating: 10   **Cost Rating: 3**
Overall Rating: 8.3
Bulk Buy

MORE RECOMMENDED RED WINE FROM NEW ZEALAND:
- Craggy Range Single Vineyard Te Kahu Hawke's Bay Gimblett Gravels Vineyard Proprietary Red
- Dashwood Marlborough Pinot Noir
- Kim Crawford Marlborough Pinot Noir
- Saint Clair Vicar's Choice Pinot Noir
- Stoneleigh Marlborough Pinot Noir
- Wairau River Marlborough Pinot Noir

Box O' Birds Sauvignon Blanc 2013—*Pure New Zealand*

Sauvignon Blanc from Marlborough, New Zealand. 12.5% Alcohol.

Suggested Retail Price: $16. Available for as low as $12.

From the bottle:

box of birds colloq somewhat curiously, this is a standard answer to the inquiry "How are you?" and signifies that the speaker is cheerful, happy or in fine health. [ORIGIN New Zealand]

Affordable New Zealand Sauvignon Blanc at its best.

Nestled deep in the South Pacific, New Zealand's wine regions enjoy a cool, dry, maritime climate ideally suited to fine wine production.

Fittingly from a country that was once ruled by birds, Box O' Birds is a selection of our finest regional varieties.

Beautifully balanced, this wine showcases the fine aromatics which New Zealand wines are renowned for. To feel a 'Box O' Birds', enjoy this wine with food and friends over the next three years.

As a remote island in the Pacific Ocean (and the world's southernmost wine-producing region), kiwis have a pioneering spirit and a style for doing things in their own, sometimes quirky, way. One of their greatest achievements in the wine world was to create a unique and extremely tasty style of Sauvignon Blanc. From the name to the aroma and taste, this wine is the perfect representation of the New Zealand style.

The **2013 Box O' Birds Sauvignon Blanc** begins with classic New Zealand Sauvignon Blanc aromas. There's lots of pleasant gooseberry, lemongrass, and tropical fruit, which all continue when tasting this crisp and tasty wine. You'll also find a fantastic lively acidity. What really sets this wine apart, however, is the excellent and very long finish. This is New Zealand Sauvignon Blanc at its best.

Taste Rating: 8   **Cost Rating: 7**

Overall Rating: 7.8

Highly Recommended

MORE RECOMMENDED WHITE WINE FROM NEW ZEALAND:
- Craggy Range Kidnappers Vineyard Hawkes Bay Chardonnay
- Craggy Range Te Muna Road Martinborough Sauvignon Blanc
- Dashwood Marlborough Sauvignon Blanc
- Kim Crawford Sauvignon Blanc
- Lay of the Land Sauvignon Blanc
- Mt. Beautiful North Canterbury Riesling
- Mud House Sauvignon Blanc
- Oyster Bay Sauvignon Blanc
- Stoneleigh Marlborough Sauvignon Blanc

SOUTH AFRICA

South Africa is another wine region making a wide assortment of excellent wines. While many of those wines tend to be over our $20 price ceiling, there are a number of value propositions to be found. Chenin Blanc is one variety that stands out and we'll call out a few of our favorites that sell for right around $10. If you're a Chardonnay drinker who hasn't tried this variety, I encourage you to check it out.

Indaba Chenin Blanc 2011—*A Steal at $7*

100% Chenin Blanc from Western Cape, South Africa. 13.5% Alcohol.

Suggested Retail Price: $10. Available for as low as $7.

From the bottle:
> Indaba is the traditional Zulu forum for sharing ideas. In this spirit we collaborate to produce great wines.
>
> This crisp, refreshing white is packed with luscious tropical fruit, citrus, and melon flavors and a touch of honey. It makes a great match for salads, light pasta dishes, mild cheeses, sushi, and seafood.
>
> World-wide sales of Indaba wines help fund the Indaba scholarship, established to open the wine industry to a new generation of South Africans.

Crisp and clean!

Chenin Blanc originated in the Loire Valley in France. In South Africa it is also known as Steen and is the most widely planted grape variety in that country, accounting for about 20 percent of all vineyard growth. Much like Chardonnay, Chenin Blanc can be made with and without the use of oak aging, producing very different wines. The Indaba goes the unoaked route and the result is quite nice. This is a fantastic wine and a steal at only $7. Stock up!

The **2011 Indaba Chenin Blanc** begins with pleasant and even complex aromas of lime, melon, guava, and other tropical fruit plus a little granny smith apple. Tasting this medium-bodied wine reveals a thick and luscious mouthfeel with crisp and clean flavors of zesty citrus and melon, nice minerality, and even a bit of spice. The crisp and clean theme continues on the lingering finish.

Taste Rating: 8   **Cost Rating: 9**

Overall Rating: 8.3

Bulk Buy

MORE RECOMMENDED WHITE WINE FROM SOUTH AFRICA:
- Bellingham Citrus Grove Chenin Blanc
- Beyond Sauvignon Blanc
- Boschendal 1685 Chardonnay-Pinot Noir
- Douglas Green The Beach House Sparkling Wine
- Douglas Green The Beach House White
- Indaba Chardonnay
- Ken Forrester Reserve Chenin Blanc
- Protea White
- Raats Original Unwooded Chenin Blanc
- Simonsig Chenin Blanc

Kanonkop Kadette 2010—
An Excellent Cuvée from the
Cape

44% Pinotage, 41% Cabernet
Sauvignon, 9% Merlot, and
6% Cabernet Franc from
Stellenbosch, South Africa.
14% Alcohol.

Suggested Retail Price: $15.
Available for as low as $11.

From the bottle:

STYLE: Full bodied—dry red
wine with a concentrated
berry, banana, cherry and
fruit flavours with a spicy finish.

Your marching orders: Drink this wine!

SERVE: At room temperature or just below room temperature.

FOOD SUGGESTIONS: Meat, pasta and spicy dishes.

GRAPES: A blend of Pinotage (44 percent), Cabernet Sauvignon
(41 percent), Merlot (9 percent), Cabernet Franc (6 percent).

ORIGIN: From the quality wine production region of Stellenbosch, east of Cape Town.

KANONKOP: Means "Canon Hill" and is derived from the days
when cannons were fired to signal the arrival of Dutch trade
ships into Cape Town Harbor.

STORAGE: Can be consumed now but should develop even further for the next five years.

The Pinotage grape was created in South Africa as a cross between
Pinot Noir and Hermitage (Cinsault) in 1925. Since then it has
become, for some, the signature grape of South Africa. Unfortunately it has had an up and down history, with many calling it an
acquired taste—that's not meant to be a compliment. Recently

however it seems to also be having a bit of a renaissance in single varietal bottlings, which I encourage you to seek out.

The **2010 Kanonkop Kadette** is a little closed at first, but as with most things in life patience is rewarded. Once the bouquet opens up you'll find excellent blackberry and plum aromas, a bit on the jammy side, plus some vanilla and smoky spice. Tasting the wine reveals a silky smooth texture and excellent juicy fruit tending more toward cranberry in the mouth but still containing blackberry and plum like the bouquet. There's also a nice layered spice component with a pleasant smokiness all the way through to the long finish. Very nice!

Taste Rating: 8   Cost Rating: 7

Overall Rating: 7.8

Highly Recommended

MORE RECOMMENDED RED WINE FROM SOUTH AFRICA:
- Arabella Shiraz
- Boschendal 1685 Shiraz
- DeMorgenzon DMZ Syrah
- Douglas Green The Beach House Red
- Excelsior Cabernet Sauvignon
- Franschhoek Cellar Stone Bridge Pinotage
- Franschhoek Cellars The Stonewalker Cabernet Sauvignon
- Glen Carlou Grand Classique
- Honey Badger Sweet Red Wine
- Lions Drift Pinotage
- Protea Red
- Thelema Mountain Red

CHAPTER 5

BUYING WINE

B Y FAR, THE SINGLE MOST popular question I get asked is, "How can I find the wine you recommend?" Unfortunately, there is no easy answer. With over 120,000 wines produced each year the average liquor store can only stock a tiny fraction, a few thousand at most. That means when you walk into any given store there are well over 110,000 other wines available that are not on the shelves! (For the reason why review Tenet #6 in our Ten Tenets of Reverse Wine Snobbery.)

While most of the wines I've discussed are popular labels that are available everywhere, I also love those hidden gems that are harder to find. Here's some advice that should help you find the wines in this book:

1. The first and easiest thing to do is to simply go into your favorite store and ask if they can order the wine you are trying to find. If it's a good store, you'll likely be surprised at what they can get for you. The better stores won't make you order a minimum quantity or charge you anything additional. You may find the independent stores more accommodating than the big chains.

2. If you'd like to check whether the wine you're looking for is available at Costco or Trader Joe's, check the Wine Ranking page at ReverseWineSnob.com. This is not foolproof, as inventory generally varies at each location, but I've compiled as much info as I can there due to its lack of availability elsewhere.

3. To locate stores that carry the wine you're looking for you can do a search on Wine-Searcher.com. Enter the wine's name, your location, and a radius; the site will tell you if any of the stores in its database have the wine in stock.

4. Check with the importer/distributor of the wine. Many importers and distributors have store locators on their websites. There may be a lot more stores carrying the wine in your area than you think. And if they don't have an online store locator, just send them an email. Most are happy to help you find their wine; that's their business.

5. If none of these options work, then it's time to buy online (if you can).

HOW TO BUY WINE ONLINE—IT'S NOT AS HARD AS YOU THINK!

For many of us online shopping has become a big part of our lives. And while buying from Amazon has become the norm, you may still be hesitant about shifting your wine buying online—after all, this is precious cargo we're talking about here! But buying wine online doesn't have to be intimidating. It can, however, take some work and has some caveats. Here are some tips and tricks that should help you begin the process painlessly.

STEP 1: CHECK YOUR STATE'S WINE SHIPMENT RULES.

For most states this is an all or nothing proposition, as states usually either allow or do not allow all wine shipments. There are, however, a few states that will allow intrastate shipments but not shipments from other states, and sometimes the rules are different by region within a state. At last count there are about thirty-nine states that allow the direct shipment of wine. The Wine Institute has lots of helpful information here.

STEP 2: MAKE SURE SOMEONE WILL BE HOME TO SIGN FOR YOUR SHIPMENT.

This is required by law in most states. UPS/FedEx will not deliver alcohol to a neighbor's house and receiving wine at work is not allowed at many companies and can be just plain awkward at others. The shipment has to be physically signed by someone at the recipient address, so if no one is home you're out of luck.

FedEx and UPS will, however, hold your package for pickup at no charge. With UPS you'll usually have to travel to one of their big shipping centers, which can be a haul for some of us while FedEx will hold it at your nearest Print and Ship office. Also be sure to sign up for the UPS MyChoice and FedEx Delivery Tracker services. Both give you the option to set up alerts to let you know a couple days before packages arrive (even if you didn't know they were coming) and allow you to reschedule delivery or hold for pickup before the first attempt.

Assuming you're comfortable with Steps 1 and 2, you probably fall into one of two groups:

A. You want to try lots of different types of wine and are just trying to find the best deals.

B. You know the wine you want and just want to find the best price.

Let's discuss the best strategies for each group.

LOOKING FOR A DEAL

If you're not concerned with the varietal or the vintage but just want to score some great wine at a great price, check out the "flash" wine sites. (Check out the Deals page on Reverse WineSnob.com to find some of our favorites.) These are sites that sell limited quantities of a wine in "flash sales." Once the wine sells out, it's gone and likely never to return. It may take a bit of waiting to find the right deal, but these sites typically offer large discounts.

One note of caution: shipping cost can be killer. To the extent you can, take advantage of large quantity buys to lower the shipping cost per bottle—or better yet, buy during promotional free shipping periods some sites offer. On ReverseWineSnob.com, I list exclusive free shipping deals from our sponsors.

KNOW WHAT YOU WANT

If you have a specific wine you're looking for, you can get a lot more precise with your search. Wine-Searcher.com is a great resource for finding the lowest price sellers (and local retailers). Most of the reviews at ReverseWineSnob.com include a link to the Wine-Searcher results page to make this super easy.

Probably the best advice I can give to the "Know What You Want" group is simply to go direct to the winery when you can. While the opportunities to do so may be limited, many wineries have member clubs that grant you special privileges. For example, wineries like Andrew Murray Vineyard or Bonny Doon Vineyard offer clubs that give discounts on wine as well as other perks like free shipping on some orders. Perhaps the best part about purchasing directly is that you know you are supporting a winery you love. The wineries themselves make more money on these orders, so you're helping to ensure they prosper and make more of their delicious vino!

A couple final considerations:

- **Temperature**—Heat is wine's worst enemy so you'll want to avoid having wine shipped when the temps are over 80 degrees. And remember, it's not just your temperature that's important but also the areas where your wine will travel. FedEx and UPS will both hold packages for you at their air conditioned locations so you can avoid wine sitting on hot delivery trucks all day.
- **Buy from a reputable source**—The last thing you want to worry about is paying for damaged shipments. Check out consumer reviews before you buy to make sure your chosen retailer is legit. Saving a couple dollars isn't worth it if the store doesn't stand behind its product.

CHAPTER 6

COSTCO

ONE OF THE KEY COMPONENTS to finding great wine for under $20 is finding the least expensive place to buy wine. The lower the markup on a wine, the better the chance we have of finding it under our $20 threshold. (Markup is the difference between the wholesale price and the retail price—it's the store's cut.) I see the exact same wine for wildly different prices at competing stores all the time, so finding the stores with the best prices in your market is critical. For many of us, one of those stores will be Costco. Here's why:

Costco's average margin (per their financial filings) is about 12 percent. Costco has stated that the highest margin they will take on a non-Costco brand is 13 percent and they strive to keep it closer to 10 percent. On private label items (Kirkland Signature) they will go up to 15 percent margin but of course the price is still lower than other brands because they cut out the middleman. It's an amazing business model—their stores average about $160 million each in annual sales. Their total revenue is around $90 billion and they make several billion in net earnings, yet investors complain because they think their margin is too low and they pay their employees too much!

So what does this have to do with buying wine? I believe the 10–13 percent margin is similar for alcohol. No wonder Costco is the largest retailer of wine in the United States. I talked to a local store manager recently and commented on how a local upscale restaurant was advertising a wine for $12 per glass and $46 per bottle. At the time my local Costco was selling this wine for $9.99

a bottle. He stated Costco's markup on that item was 12 percent, which would put their margin at just under 11 percent. This means that unless you're dealing with a special buy/closeout type situation, you really are not going to find wine much cheaper than at Costco.

The other nice thing about Costco is that in my experience their buyers do a fantastic job picking out high-quality products. If they stock it, you can be fairly sure it's good, unlike some of the other big chain stores. Since Costco is the largest retailer of wine in the United States, products tend to turn over quickly so there is quite a variety over time. The downside of this is that a wine you loved may be gone the next week, so if you like it you better buy a bunch.

One other note on Costco is that typically any price that ends in .97 is a markdown. Furthermore, if there is an asterisk on the label that means it is a closeout and is not coming back. In most areas, markdowns are not common in the liquor store, but they do occur so keep any eye out for them! (This is a great tip for shopping the rest of the store too. Costco doesn't advertise sale or clearance prices but if you see a price ending in .97 that means it has in fact been marked down. We've picked up some awesome deals on marked-down items throughout the store.)

My rule of thumb is to buy any wines that are widely available at Costco as well as their excellent Kirkland Signature brand wines. These are wines that Costco sources themselves from premium producers but sells at a deep discount. Here is a list of a few of our top Kirkland Signature picks. Hopefully you'll all be able to find at least a few of these at your local store.

Kirkland Signature Rutherford Napa Valley Meritage 2012—*Revisiting an Old Friend*

58% Merlot, 26% Cabernet Sauvignon, 8% Petit Verdot, 6% Cabernet Franc, and 2% Malbec from Rutherford, Napa Valley, California. 14.9% Alcohol.

Available for $13.99 exclusively at Costco.

From the bottle:
> The Napa Valley, Rutherford AVA is known for its unique terroir of volcanic-influenced soil laced with gravel, sand, and loam.
> Deep, concentrated, black cherry notes are surrounded by ripe black currant, cinnamon and sweet oak spice. The lifting acidity frames the rich fruit and the classic 'Rutherford Dust.'"—Winemakers Marco DiGiulio & Glenn Hugo

This wine is one we have enjoyed immensely over the last few years, offering a chance to sample wine from the prestigious Rutherford AVA in Napa Valley. In fact, this area is so renowned that there are almost no other red wines under $20 produced here.

The **2012 Kirkland Signature Rutherford Napa Valley Meritage** begins with pleasant aromas of black cherry, plum, blackberry, licorice, and a little baking spice. The wine tastes nice but is a bit more one dimensional than previous vintages. You'll find loads of jammy fruit and other flavors quite similar to the nose. Dry, grippy tannins lead into the medium-long finish, which still features that trademark dusty texture known as "Rutherford dust."

Taste Rating: 8   **Cost Rating: 6**

Overall Rating: 7.5

Recommended Buy

Kirkland Signature Sonoma County Old Vine Zinfandel 2011—*Classic Zin at a Great Costco Price*

Zinfandel from Sonoma Valley, California. 15.3% Alcohol.

Available for $10.99 exclusively at Costco.

From the bottle:
This estate-produced Zinfandel comes from a collection of archival vineyards that have been home to Zinfandel for more than 150 years. Kirkland Signature Old Vine Zinfandel is produced from low-yielding vines that average 45 years of age. This classic Old Vine Zinfandel has opaque shades of deep red-purple fruit with a bouquet and palate structure of blackberry, cassis, blueberry and chocolate, which is supported by vanilla and spice notes from oak maturation and lifted by bright acidity and supple, ripe tannins.

Quite a flavorful wine for just $11.

The **2011 Kirkland Signature Sonoma County Old Vine Zinfandel** begins with aromas of black cherry, bramble, a bit of coffee, spice, and some nice floral notes. Tasting the wine reveals a great example of a Sonoma Zin with brambly flavors of ripe black cherry, blackberry, blueberry, and cranberry. You'll also find a bit of leathery spice and vanilla in this very flavorful wine. It ends with more ripe fruit, leather, and spice that lingers for a good amount of time.

Taste Rating: 8   **Cost Rating: 7**

Overall Rating: 7.8

Highly Recommended

Kirkland Signature Côtes du Rhône Villages 2011— *A Whole Lot of Complexity For $7*

A blend of Syrah, Grenache, and Mourvedre from Côtes du Rhône Villages, France. 14% Alcohol.

Available for $6.99 exclusively at Costco.

From the bottle:
Only one-fifth of the wine produced in Southern Rhone's Côtes du Rhône qualifies for the superior designation of Côtes du Rhône Villages. Vintner Patrick Leset is recognized among the top winemakers in the region, and his wines are among the finest in France. He brings decades of experience in the Rhone to this Kirkland Signature Côtes du Rhône Villages.

Syrah delivers the deep black fruit concentration and smooth chocolate. Grenache adds balanced harmony, warmth and fruit-forward notes of black plum and blackberry. Mourvedre gives the sense of sweet earth to this classic blend from the Rhone.—Patrick Leset, Winemaker.

The **2011 Kirkland Signature Côtes du Rhône Villages** begins with intriguing aromas of deep, dark fruit, spice, and excellent earthy notes—much more than you would expect to find in your typical $7 wine. The wine tastes very oaky when first opened but that quickly dissipates to reveal tons of dark, jammy fruit counterbalanced by those excellent earthy notes. Licorice, oak, and spice round things out. It ends dry, earthy, and oaky with good length.

This wine offers a whole lot of complexity for such a low price, and it's even better on day two.

Taste Rating: 8   **Cost Rating: 9**
Overall Rating: 8.3
Bulk Buy

Kirkland Signature Malbec 2011—*Plenty Good, but it's not a Pop and Pour Proposition*

100% Malbec from Mendoza, Argentina. 13.5% Alcohol.

Available for $6.99 exclusively at Costco.

From the bottle:
> In the heart of Argentina's most important and acclaimed wine producing region lies Mendoza, known as "the land of sun and wine." This high-altitude region extends from 2,000 to over 5,000 feet above sea level and is the source of Kirkland Signature Malbec. Intense sunlight and sandy soil, coupled with cool temperatures, result in an extended ripening cycle to balance sugar and acidity. The Malbec is aged for 12 months in oak barrels, adding complexity, balance, and structure to this full-bodied wine. Drink now through 2016.

The **2011 Kirkland Signature Malbec** begins with pleasant aromas of smoky ripe fruit and spice. Tasting the wine reveals smooth flavors of plum, blackberry, and spice and also a good degree of oak influence right now. It's most noticeable on the finish, which features lots of toasty, burnt oak notes. That domination definitely lessens with a good bit of air, so you'll definitely want to give this wine time to breathe if you drink it now. Stick it in the cellar for a year or two and you should be rewarded nicely.

Taste Rating: 7   **Cost Rating: 9**

Overall Rating: 7.5

Recommended Buy

Kirkland Signature Bordeaux Superieur 2010—*A Bordeaux Bargain*

70% Merlot and 30% Cabernet Sauvignon from Bordeaux, France. 13.5% Alcohol.

Available for $6.99 exclusively at Costco.

From the bottle:

Chateau Le Gardera is a fine producer of Bordeaux Superieur wines and an outstanding source for this 2010 Kirkland Signature wine. Bordeaux Superieur, an appellation that covers the same geographical area as Bordeaux AOC, is known for smaller yields. The property is situated on slopes to the south of St. Emilion, overlooking the Garonne River. A carefully selected blend of 70 percent Merlot and 30 percent Cabernet Sauvignon was aged twelve months in Allier French oak barrels creating a luscious, well-balanced, and easy-drinking wine that exudes finesse. The high-quality fruit has aromas of ripe cherries, blackcurrant berries and subtle toasted notes, which flow to a generous palate and silky tannins. Drink now through 2016.

The **2010 Kirkland Signature Bordeaux Superieur** begins with a very nice aroma of plum, blackcurrant, and spice plus a little vanilla and toasty oak. Tasting this medium-bodied wine reveals a smooth texture, lots of juicy black cherry and other ripe berry flavors, and more toasty oak. The oak dissipates with some air so consider decanting before serving. It finishes dry with more dark fruit and a bit of oak that resolves into tobacco notes at the very end. Quite a deal for only $7!

Taste Rating: 7   Cost Rating: 9

Overall Rating: 7.5

Recommended Buy

MORE RECOMMENDED KIRKLAND SIGNATURE WINE:
- Kirkland Signature Chateauneuf du Pape
- Kirkland Signature Marlborough Sauvignon Blanc
- Kirkland Signature Napa Valley Meritage
- Kirkland Signature Prosecco
- Kirkland Signature Rioja Reserva
- Kirkland Signature Russian River Pinot Noir
- Kirkland Signature Series Malbec
- Kirkland Signature Series Russian River Chardonnay

CHAPTER 7

TRADER JOE'S

WHETHER FOOD OR WINE, TRADER Joe's concentrates on creating private label items that are unique to their company. This represents a very different business model than Costco. In fact, 80 percent of the items that Trader Joe's sells are private label, which simply means they contract directly with the original producer to make a product to their own specifications. That product then carries the Trader Joe's name (or some other brand name they create) instead of the original producer's. Although they don't actually label many of the wines they sell as a Trader Joe's brand most can only be purchased there. Unlike Costco, Trader Joes dominates by driving down their product costs through their buying power and cutting out the middlemen. In addition, there's also almost no marketing cost (a substantial part of what you're paying for in many products) since Trader Joe's does virtually no advertising. This allows them to sell products cheaply but still maintain a good amount of margin.

What you will notice, however, is that the non-Trader Joe's wines are generally not priced very competitively. For example, I once found a Coppola Claret that could be purchased for $10 at Costco selling for $17 at Trader Joe's. What gives? It's all part of the Trader Joe's pricing strategy.

Basically Trader Joe's is all about selling their own wine since they make the most money on their private label items. The general market wines are really just there to make their own prices look better. By pricing the general market wines high and their own labels low, it reinforces the perception of value on the Trader

Joe's exclusive wines (and really on all their private label items). One local distributor I talked to said that this means few of their general market producers really have any desire to be in Trader Joe's, as they are just there to look bad. (They're even often placed in the least desirable shelf space, the very bottom row.) This is very different than Costco where producers often bite the bullet and take the lower than usual margins because there is so much potential volume.

Go to Trader Joe's for great deals on their exclusive wines under $10.

Trader Joe's GSM Reserve Lot# 96 2012—*Three of My Favorite Letters*

52% Syrah, 38% Grenache, and 10% Mourvèdre from Dry Creek Valley, Sonoma, California. 14.5% Alcohol.

Available for $9.99 exclusively at Trader Joe's.

From the bottle:
Bright strawberry, cherry, and raspberry notes with hints of spice and vanilla oak leading to an exceptionally well-balanced finish.

The GSM label in this wine comes from the blend of Grenache, Syrah, and Mourvedre. This combination was made famous in the Southern Rhone Valley of France and can now be found all over the world. This example from Trader Joe's comes from one of our favorite spots, Dry Creek Valley in California.

The **2012 Trader Joe's GSM Reserve Lot# 96 Dry Creek Valley** begins with a pleasant aroma of strawberry, black cherry, spice, a little vanilla, smoked meat, and even a few earthy notes. Tasting this medium-bodied wine reveals lots of tasty, juicy black cherry, blackberry, and plum. It ends dry with medium-long length and lingering fruit and spice notes. This wine is mighty fun to drink and has fairly good complexity to boot, just the way we like it.

Taste Rating: 8   **Cost Rating: 8**

Overall Rating: 8.0

Highly Recommended

Il Tarocco Chianti Classico 2011—*Classic Chianti Classico for under $10*

90% Sangiovese and 10% Canaiolo Nero from Tuscany, Italy. 13.5% Alcohol.

Available for $9.99 exclusively at Trader Joe's.

From the bottle:
Made from carefully selected Sangiovese (90 percent) and Canaiolo Nero (10 percent) grapes. This wine has intense ruby color and aromas of ripe red fruit. This is a full, well-balanced wine with a nice finish.

Aged in small oak french barrels for twelve months and six months in the bottle to acquire smoothness.

Serve at room temperature with roasted beef, pork or lamb dishes.

The **2011 Torraccia di Presura Il Tarocco Chianti Classico** begins with the classic sour red and black cherry Sangiovese aromas, leather, and spice. Tasting reveals a rustic wine (just like a good Chianti should be) with more savory sour black cherry, leather notes, and a fairly prominent earthy undertone. The wine needs a couple hours to open up but when it does you'll find a great example of a Chianti Classico at a fabulous price. Dry, grippy tannins lead into the medium-long finish.

Taste Rating: 7   **Cost Rating: 8**

Overall Rating: 7.3

Recommended Buy

Panilonco Merlot Malbec Reserva 2012—*Surprisingly drinkable for only $4.99*

60% Merlot and 40% Malbec from Colchagua Valley, Chile. 13% Alcohol.

Available for $4.99 exclusively at Trader Joe's.

From the bottle:

> This smooth red combines the ripe fruit flavours of Merlot with the rich blackberry notes of Malbec to give an intensely fruity, soft full flavoured wine.
>
> Delicious on its own, this wine is the perfect partner for roast lamb, steak, barbecued meats or with cheese.

While we're all about cheap wine, we're also realistic. There's plenty of really bad cheap wine out there, especially when you start talking about wine under $5. It's amazingly hard to make a quality wine for a price that low—the cost of the bottle, cork, and label alone eat up a good chunk of that $5. Add in the cost of shipping, which is all the way from Chile in the case of this wine, and there's not much left.

And all this doesn't even factor in the cost of the wine itself, the most important part! And then there's the awful three-tier distribution system in our country, which fills distributors' pockets at the expense of consumers and the wineries themselves. Add to that the retailer's margin and it begins to boggle the mind that a wine could possibly be priced so low.

All this to say that when we find a good, quality wine that is able to overcome all these obstacles and sell at such a low price point we have to give it props, even if it's not rocketing to the top of our rating scale. But that's the beauty of our unique rating system—because it only costs $5 it doesn't have to score as high of a Taste rating as a wine that costs $15 in order to qualify as a recommended buy.

The **2012 Panilonco "Chief of Lions" Merlot Malbec Reserva** from the Errazuriz Ovalle Family and Vinedos Marchigue begins with pleasant aromas of plum and other ripe dark fruit including a little cranberry and a bit of wintergreen. This easy-drinking, medium-bodied wine tastes smooth and simple with lots of plum, blackberry, and grape jam along with a hint of spice and even a few earthy notes. It could use a little more acidity and a longer finish but for $4.99 this is a surprisingly drinkable wine that is likely to be a crowd-pleaser.

Taste Rating: 6   **Cost Rating: 10**
Overall Rating: 7.0
Recommended Buy

Picton Bay South Island Pinot Noir 2013—*A Pinot Noir for the 99*

Pinot Noir from Marlborough and Nelson, South Island, New Zealand. 13.5% Alcohol.

Available for $7.99 exclusively at Trader Joe's.

From the bottle:
> This wine is made from grapes grown in Marlborough and Nelson. Picton Bay Pinot Noir is fresh with delicious red fruit flavours, enticing aromas and a smooth, fine texture. Drink now or cellar until 2016.

In our opinion there's way too much overpriced Pinot Noir out there. Unfortunately, inexpensive and easy-drinking bottles are hard to come by, so when we find them we like to call them out with the "Pinot Noir for the 99" label. And this wine from Trader Joe's fits the bill perfectly.

The **2013 Picton Bay South Island Pinot Noir** begins with pleasant aromas of black and red cherry, spice, licorice, and strawberry with a hint of earth. Tasting this easy drinking light-to-medium-bodied wine reveals similar flavors of red and black cherry, a nice bit of spice, and some cola notes. We love New Zealand Pinot Noir because of the fantastic value. This bottle is half or less of what you would normally pay for a wine of this quality from New Zealand, which is in turn less than half of what you'd pay for the same quality from Oregon or California.

For me where a lot of cheap Pinot Noir falls apart is the lack any well-developed spice notes and/or the finish, and this wine does well in both categories. At only $8 this is a Bulk Buy! Give it a couple hours to decant to experience it at its best.

Taste Rating: 8   **Cost Rating: 9**

Overall Rating: 8.3

Bulk Buy

Rosa dell'Olmo Barbera d'Asti 2011—*Budget Barbera!*

Barbera from Barbera d'Asti, Asti, Piedmont, Italy. 13% Alcohol.

Available for $5.49 exclusively at Trader Joe's.

From the bottle:
An everyday and easy to drink red wine. Deep ruby red in color, with pleasant and distinctive red fruit notes, it is dry and rich and has a remarkable silky texture.

A darn good wine for the price.

The **2011 Rosa dell'Olmo Barbera d'Asti** begins with a nice aroma of black cherry, spice, leather, and a bit of an earthy note. Tasting reveals lots of juicy black cherry, plum, maraschino cherry, and strawberry wrapped up in a smooth and easy-to-drink texture. There's also good acidity and well-integrated spice in this light-to medium-bodied wine. It ends with a hint of earthiness and surprising length for a wine this inexpensive. It might not be the prototypical example of the variety but this is one enjoyable wine.

Taste Rating: 7   **Cost Rating: 10**
Overall Rating: 7.8
Highly Recommended

Trader Joe's Grand Reserve Napa Valley Meritage 2011—*Easily Worth Twice the Price*

Meritage from Napa Valley, California. 13.8% Alcohol.

Available for $12.99 exclusively at Trader Joe's.

No info on bottle.

As we stated earlier, we're big fans of Meritage blends and this is a nice one. The **2011**

Trader Joe's Grand Reserve Lot 27 Napa Valley Meritage begins with an excellent and complex aroma of blackberry, plum, a little spice, tobacco, and lots of fabulous vanilla and caramel notes. All of those same flavors are evident when tasting this smooth, lush, and delicious medium, to full-bodied wine. Give it a couple hours to decant to really enjoy it at its best. A little spice leads into the dry, long finish that features plenty more vanilla, caramel, and even a little chocolate under the lingering juicy fruit. This is a fantastic wine that is easily worth twice the price.

Taste Rating: 9   **Cost Rating: 6**

Overall Rating: 8.3

Bulk Buy

Monte Ducay Reserva 2009—*An Excellent Pick from an Often Overlooked Region*

A blend of Tempranillo, Garnacha, and Cabernet Sauvignon from Carinena, Aragon, Spain. 13% Alcohol.

Available for $6.99 exclusively at Trader Joe's.

From the bottle:
Monte Ducay vineyard is located in a beautiful landscape, with stony, sandy and light soils. It produces very well balanced wines, with pronounced colour and distinctive character.

Tasting Notes: Beautiful cherry red tinted with brick overtones. Fragrant and delicate on the nose. Elegant bouquet, generous and well balanced. Long, lingering aftertaste.

Oak Aging: 14 months in American oak followed by 24 months in the bottle.

One of the beauties of Trader Joe's is their ability to find inexpensive gems, and one of the ways they do this is to source wine from some lesser-known regions. This wine is a perfect case in point.

The Carinena region in northern Spain is just northeast of one of our favorite value regions in the whole world—the Calatayud. And like the Calatayud, winemaking here goes back to the Roman times. The area is also known for its rocky soils and high elevations, a fabulous combination for growing flavorful grapes. Because the area doesn't have the same name recognition as, say, Rioja or Ribera Del Duero, there is great value to be found.

The **2009 Bodegas San Valero Monte Ducay Reserva** begins with abundant aromas of baking spice (nutmeg, allspice, cinnamon, and vanilla) plus ripe red cherry and plum. It smells great and is surprisingly complex for the price, no doubt due to the fourteen months of aging in American oak. Tasting the medium-bodied wine reveals super ripe, dark, rich, and juicy fruit with great depth of flavor. There's also decent acidity and an ultrasmooth texture. Wonderful spicy notes kick in midpalate along with some nice graphite minerality that lasts all the way into the medium-long, dry finish. Excellent!

Taste Rating: 8   **Cost Rating: 9**
Overall Rating: 8.3
Bulk Buy

Grifone Primitivo 2012—
Super Grape Jam!

Primitivo (Zinfandel) from Puglia, Italy. 13% Alcohol.

Available for $3.99 exclusively at Trader Joe's.

From the bottle:

Zinfandel in America . . . Primitivo in Italy . . . Mali Plavac in Croatia . . . For more than a millenium, the mystery grape of international viticulture travelled all over the world. Grifone is 100 percent Primitivo from old Zinfandel vines of Puglia region, a result of long study made in conjunction with local growers, trying to rediscover the original concentration of fruit, spices and flavours of this historical grape. Our Primitivo is soft and deep with flavorful vanilla notes and a long finish.

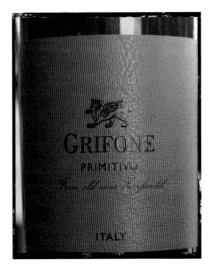

Surprisingly good for only $3.99 and a great label for your Halloween parties or hunting trips.

This is another Trader Joe's exclusive wine that falls into what seems to be their sweet spot—cheap Italian wine. And while California may be the first region to come to mind when thinking of old vine Zinfandel, Italy also has its share; you just may not realize it since it is called Primitivo there. Regardless, old vine anything for only $3.99 raises our eyebrows and so it was with a heavy dose of skepticism that we gave this wine a try.

The **2012 Grifone Primitivo** begins with pleasant aromas of cherry, cranberry, spearmint, and a little spice. The wine tastes surprisingly not bad for only $4 with a lot of typical Zinfandel qualities. On our first sip we were a bit overwhelmed by all the grape jam, but we liked it more and more the longer it was open.

With air, the wine reveals maraschino and sour cherry flavors, cranberry, strawberry, vanilla, a hint of bramble, and a little spice that flows into the dry, tart berry-infused finish. Just like many other Zins this one would make a nice match for anything drenched in BBQ sauce, and with its bright orange label it makes a great fit for your Halloween parties and hunting trips.

Taste Rating: 7   **Cost Rating: 10**
Overall Rating: 7.8
Highly Recommended

Pasqua Ripasso Valpolicella Superiore 2011—*Hits the Trifecta*

A blend of Corvina, Rondinella, and Molinara from Veneto, Italy. 13.5% Alcohol.

Available for $8.99 exclusively at Trader Joe's.

From the bottle:
This wine is obtained from the 'Ripasso' technique, a secondary fermentation of the wine on the dried skins of the grapes already used to make appassimento wines. Aged in wooden barrels for 8 months before being bottled. A full-bodied wine, with an intense bouquet of wild cherries and redcurrant, well recommended for roast meat and mature cheese. Serve at 18C.

This Trader Joe's exclusive wine is complex, easy to drink, *and* cheap!

As mentioned on the label, this wine is made in the Ripasso style, a process that has become quite popular in Valpolicella wines. Typically grapes are dried for many weeks, allowing the sugars to concentrate and become more powerful. These dried grapes are used to make Amarone wines but then the leftover grape pomace is effectively recycled by refermenting it with standard Valpolicella wine. The goal is to add depth and complexity to a wine that is normally quite light-bodied. To get the Superiore designation like this wine, the wine must also be aged at least one year.

    The **2011 Pasqua Ripasso Valpolicella Superiore** begins with pleasant aromas of maraschino cherry, sour cherry, strawberry, and some dried herbs. The medium-bodied wine tastes of red currant, raisins, cherry, and spicy oak with undertones of dried herbs. It also has a bit of a rustic quality to it, which I enjoy. Overall this wine is that rare combination of being easy to drink and complex—the best of both worlds. Add in the cheap price and you've hit the trifecta! It ends sweet and savory with good length. This wine would be a nice match with lots of different rustic Italian dishes.

Taste Rating: 8   **Cost Rating: 8**
Overall Rating: 8.0
Highly Recommended

Berton Vineyard The Black Shiraz 2011—*The Epitome of a Great Trader Joe's Wine*

Shiraz from Barossa, Australia. 14% Alcohol.

Available for $7.49 exclusively at Trader Joe's.

From the bottle:

> The Black Barossa Shiraz is a partnership between some of the Barossa Valley's pioneering grape growing families dating back to the 1840's with distinctive individual soil characteristics, that is recognized throughout the world as one of the best grape growing regions for Shiraz. This Barossa Shiraz is a tribute to its heritage, allowing us to produce a full flavoured wine. Inky black in colour with rich dark fruit cake characters, combining hints of black pepper, juicy plums and blueberries. The palate delivers great flavor, length and weight, which follows through with soft firm lingering tannins.

This wine is easy in every aspect—easy on the wallet and easy on the tastebuds; heck, it's even easy to open and ready to drink right away! Plus, how can I not like a wine that brings to mind a great Spinal Tap quote? ("It's like, how much more black could this be? And the answer is none. None more black.") But of course, like all the best wines at Trader Joe's, this one is not consistently in stock so it may take a few visits to find it. When you do, stock up!

The **2011 Berton Vineyard The Black Shiraz** begins with pleasant aromas of dark berries, spice, and a little dark chocolate. This oh-so-smooth wine tastes wonderful with lots of rich fruit, excellent spice, and great balance. And at the end where most inexpensive wines fall short, this one excels with a fantastically long finish featuring more fruit and spice. A fine example of an Australian Shiraz at a smoking price!

Taste Rating: 8   Cost Rating: 9

Overall Rating: 8.3

Bulk Buy

Dr. Beckermann Piesporter Michelsberg Spatlese Riesling and the Espiral Vinho Verde—*Cheap and Delightful White Wines*

First up is the **2012 Dr. Beckermann Piesporter Michelsberg Spatlese Riesling** from Mosel, Germany. 9% Alcohol.

Available for $6.99 exclusively at Trader Joe's.

The wine begins with aromas of green apple, honey, and some pleasant floral notes. The wine tastes simple and relatively sweet but it doesn't overdo it. This is a very easy-to-drink wine that would make a good aperitif or a nice pairing for spicy food. It could use a bit more acidity but it has really nice flavor. The low alcohol percent is also rather refreshing. It ends with a surprisingly long finish. When you break down the parts of this wine it's not all that impressive yet I couldn't help but enjoy it. This would be great wine for the end of a long, hot day on the porch!

Taste Rating: 7   **Cost Rating: 9**
Overall Rating: 7.5
Recommended Buy

Next up is the **Espiral Vinho Verde**, a nonvintage wine from Portugal. 9% Alcohol.

Available for $4.49 exclusively at Trader Joe's.

The **Espiral Vinho Verde** begins with lots of citrus on the nose, as well as some bread dough aromas. Drinking this wine is honestly a bit like having a 7-Up or Sprite thanks to all the bubbles and tons of citrus flavors. Still, it's crisp and refreshing and in the right

Espiral Vinho Verde.

situation it would certainly hit the spot. This is 90+-degree wine!

Taste Rating: 6   **Cost Rating: 10**

Overall Rating: 7.0

Recommended Buy

Cantina Del Grifone 1967 Toscana 2009—*A Perfect Partner for Pizza!*

85% Sangiovese, 10% Cabernet Sauvignon, and 5% Syrah from Tuscany, Italy. 12.5% Alcohol.

Available for $5.99 exclusively at Trader Joe's.

From the bottle:

In 1967, one year before I was born and two years before Woodstock and the first Moon-walking, my uncle Giorgio blended the first Toscana using a special ageing method that is still used today in our Grifone cellar to obtain a fruity, soft and smooth Sangiovese based "Supertuscan" from grapes selected on the Tyrrhenian coastal vineyards.

The **2009 Cantina Del Grifone 1967 Toscana** catches your attention the moment you uncork it thanks to the very strong and pleasant aromas of red and black fruit, a little black pepper, spice, and some nice violet notes. Tasting the wine reveals more fruit with the spice and other components taking a backseat. Strawberry and black cherry stand out among the abundance of red and black fruit flavors as well as a hint of red licorice. This soft and smooth wine is actually rather one dimensional—it's all about the fruit—but it works, and especially so when paired with a pizza. At only $5.99 you really can't ask for much more than this wine delivers. It ends with some mild oaky notes on the medium-length finish.

Taste Rating: 7   **Cost Rating: 10**

Overall Rating: 7.8

Highly Recommended

Pontificis GSM Blend 2011—*A GSM Blend for the Masses!*

50% Grenache, 30% Syrah, and 20% Mourvedre from Vin Pays d'Oc, Languedoc-Roussillon, France. 13.5% Alcohol.

Available for $6.99 exclusively at Trader Joe's.

From the bottle:

Produced in the Languedoc-Roussillon, between sea and mountain, from the three local grape varieties Grenache (50 percent), Syrah (30 percent) and Mourvedre (20 percent), Pontificis is deep purple in colour, with aromas of spice, black fruits and herbs and a palate of supple, yet rich spicy fruit. It is a beautiful representation of the best of the South of France.

Enjoy at 64F with meats in sauce, mediterranean dishes, marinated game and cheeses.

The **2011 Badet Clement Pontificis GSM Blend** begins with pleasant aromas of dark red fruit, a few oaky notes, menthol, and some light herbal notes. I also got a touch of heat on the nose, which is surprising given this wine is only 13.5 percent alcohol. Tasting the wine reveals more dark fruit along with leather, tobacco, and oak notes. It's a bit rough but still quite good and enjoyable to drink. It ends dry with good length and lingering tobacco notes. Overall it's a nice GSM blend at an even nicer price.

Taste Rating: 7   Cost Rating: 9

Overall Rating: 7.5

Recommended Buy

Sauvignon Republic Cellars Sauvignon Blanc 2013—*A Mouthful of Luscious Tropical Fruit, Citrus, and Honey*

Sauvignon Blanc from Marlborough, New Zealand. 13% Alcohol.

Available for $7.99 exclusively at Trader Joe's.

From the bottle:

A windswept terroir of hills and dry gravelly-clay riverbeds produces crisp tropical sauvignon with gooseberry notes, herbal grassiness, and restrained minerality. Juicy flavors, crisp acidity and long finish pair well with sea foods of all kinds. The perfect wine with Sushi!

We've long been fans of wine from New Zealand—and not just Sauvignon Blanc or Pinot Noir. A Merlot-based blend, for example, is one of our favorites. That said, the Sauvignon Blanc and Pinot Noir are darn tasty and this wine is an excellent example of New Zealand Sauvignon Blanc . . . sans the famed cat pee aromas.

The **2013 Sauvignon Republic Cellars Sauvignon Blanc** begins with classic New Zealand Sauvignon Blanc aromas like tropical fruit, lemongrass, and a little honeysuckle. Tasting reveals more tropical fruit plus a whole lot of citrus soaked in luscious honey. This is a smooth, flavorful, fresh wine with good acidity. It ends crisp with medium length. A wine that makes your mouth happy!

Taste Rating: 7   **Cost Rating: 9**

Overall Rating: 7.5

Recommended Buy

The Sommavite Brunello di Montalcino Annata and the Rocca dell'Olmo Barbaresco—*Brunello and Barbaresco on the Cheap*

First up is the **2008 Sommavite Brunello di Montalcino Annata**. This wine is 100% Sangiovese from Montalcino, Tuscany, Italy. 14.5% Alcohol.

Available for $13.99 exclusively at Trader Joe's.

From the bottle:

> Recognized as a "Four Star" vintage, our 2008 Sommavite Brunello exhibits the pure fruit of dark cherries, dried berries and flowers followed by a full-bodied yet silky finish. We suggest opening the bottle an hour in advance and matching with hearty cuisine.

The **2008 Sommavite Brunello di Montalcino Annata** certainly starts off right. Abundant aromas of dark fruit, dried herbs, and some spice combine to create a very attractive nose. Tasting the wine reveals a smooth and silky texture with dark, sour fruit. The tannins are soft and dry. There's not a lot of complexity here, but it is certainly tasty. On the finish the dark fruit turns even more sour. I'm sure Brunello aficionados could pick this one apart, but the bottom line is that for $14 this is quite a nice wine (and less than one-third the cost of a normal Brunello).

Taste Rating: 8   **Cost Rating: 6**

Overall Rating: 7.5

Recommended Buy

Next up is the 2009 Rocca dell'Olmo Barbaresco.

100% Nebbiolo from Piedmont, Italy. 13.5% Alcohol.

Available for $9.99 exclusively at Trader Joe's.

From the bottle:
> Barbaresco is a distinguished and aristocratic red wine. Ruby-red shading to garnet in color, it is very intense and forward with scents of violet and vanilla. Rich and generous in the mouth, with an elegant and lingering finish.

Trader Joe's doesn't normally reveal the producers of its exclusive wines but a web search revealed that the label was trademarked by Terre da Vino, a cooperative of three thousand growers representing almost fifteen thousand acres of vineyards in Piedmont, Italy. It doesn't look like they have many wines available in the United States but the few that do make their way here are not cheap.

The **2009 Rocca dell'Olmo Barbaresco** begins with a pleasant aroma of black cherry and spice along with a little licorice and a hint of leather. This medium-bodied wine tastes soft and easy to drink with fine, dusty tannins and lots of savory red and black cherry. It also has good acidity, which would help to make it a very good food wine. It ends dry, with good length and long-lingering spice notes. While I haven't tasted a ton of Barbaresco in my lifetime (since it is typically out of our price range), I have had a lot of $10 wine and this is one damn tasty bottle for that price. And as good as this wine is, don't bother with the $20 Barolo from the same label—it's not up to nearly the same standard.

Taste Rating: 9   **Cost Rating: 8**

Overall Rating: 8.8

Bulk Buy

Cocobon, Trentatre Rosso and the Epicuro Salice Salentino Riserva—*Trader Joe's Classics*

Trader Joe's is known for their rabid fans, and their wine selection definitely has its devotees. Here are three classic wines that have been around for years, but even today generate tons of buzz.

First up is the 2011 Cocobon Red Wine.

A wine that is such a reliable seller that the stores in my area have to restock this wine more than once a day. The wine is a blend of 61% Zinfandel, 17% Cabernet Franc, 12% Merlot, 6% Petite Verdot, and 4% Petite Sirah from California. 12.5% Alcohol.

Available for $7.99 exclusively at Trader Joe's.

From the bottle:

> We've blended our favorite Bordeaux style varietals into a rich, silky wine with a soft, luxurious finish. Delight in aromas of ripe cherries and hints of sumptuous mocha that will fill your senses. Pair with roasted lamb or mint coulis or even a dark chocolate souffle to deliver that zen moment we all need.
>
> Nirvana in a glass.

This wine is made by Georgetta Dane who took over the wine-making duties at The Big House Wines after Randall Grahm left. (He's now with Bonny Doon Vineyards.) And even though this is not my favorite type of wine (a sweet red) it is well made and should be well appreciated by fans of this style.

The **2011 Cocobon Red Wine** begins with a heady aroma full of oaky notes—vanilla, caramel, and chocolate—plus red cherry and blackberry fruit. The wine tastes smooth and sweet with similar flavors to the nose. It's easy to see why this wine is so popular as it is both easy to drink and very flavorful. The finish is medium-short and full of more sweet oak. This is a wine that should appeal greatly to all of the Apothic Red fans out there.

Taste Rating: 7   **Cost Rating: 9**

Overall Rating: 7.5

Recommended Buy

Next up is a wine that has seen moments of greatness, the 2011 Trentatre Rosso 33.

As always this wine is a blend of 33% Cabernet Sauvignon, 33% Merlot, and 33% Montepulciano from Apulia, Italy. 14% Alcohol. Available for $5.99 exclusively at Trader Joe's.

We were huge fans of the 2008 vintage but the 2009 vintage let us down. That's one of the characteristics that makes these Trader Joe's wine classics—while every vintage is reliably good for the price, every few years they hit one out of the park and really reinforce their cult status.

From the bottle:

This unique wine comes from the Apulia Region located in the depth of Southern Italy. The blend is an equal amount of three different varietals. Cabernet Sauvignon 33,3 percent, Merlot

33,3 percent, and Montepulciano 33,4 percent collectively aged six months in oak barrels, hence the name "Trentatre" which in Italian means Thirtythree. The color is a deep purple-red with a pleasant fruity nose with hints of plum, cherry, and chocolate. Full bodied, it has a supple finish with soft tannins. Enjoy it with pasta, pizza, grilled meats, seasoned cheese . . . or even on its own!

The **2011 Trentatre Rosso 33** begins with pleasant aromas of plum and a little smoke. Tasting the wine reveals sour fruit, lots of oak, a little licorice, and a smooth texture, but that's about it for this relatively simple wine. The finish is dry and of medium length. While it's certainly good enough for only $5.99 it's not the same as the vaunted 2008 (and 2007) vintages.

Taste Rating: 6   Cost Rating: 10
Overall Rating: 7.0
Recommended Buy

Lastly we have the 2009 Epicuro Salice Salentino Riserva.

A blend of 80% Negroamaro and 20% Malvasia Nera from Salice Salentino, Apulia, Italy. 13% Alcohol.

Available for $5.99 exclusively at Trader Joe's. There are a number of different Epicuro wines including a Nero d'Avola and a Primitivo, but this seems to be the one that is most well liked year in and year out.

From the bottle:

A blend of Negroamaro 80 percent and Malvasia Nera 20 percent. Intense ruby red in color with orange reflections on the outside rim of the wine. Intense and persistent aromas of red, woodsy berries. On the palate the wine is dry, well balanced, and full bodied with a long finish. Serve at room temperature with rustic meat dishes.

The **2009 Epicuro Salice Salentino Riserva** begins with pleasant aromas of ripe red berries, licorice, and oak. You'll want to give this one some time to breathe before tasting as the oak is a bit overwhelming at first. Once it has some air, there is a lot to enjoy here with the flavors in the mouth similar to the nose. Pair it with a pizza or pasta in red sauce to get the maximum enjoyment out of it.

Taste Rating: 6   Cost Rating: 10
Overall Rating: 7.0
Recommended Buy

Four Favorite Trader Joe's Picks

One of the great things about Trader Joe's is the abundance of cheap, and I mean really cheap, wine. Unfortunately a lot of it is bad, and I mean really bad.

So to round out our chapter on Trader Joe's exclusive wines, here are four of our favorites priced at $5.99 or less. These wines won't blow your socks off, but they are certainly solid and offer some good quality at such a low price. And while these are reviews of the last available vintage at the time of this writing, all four have been pretty consistent over the years so they are about as close to a safe bet as you can get for around $5.

First up is the 2013 Grifone Sangiovese from Puglia, Italy. (Grifone is pronounced Gree-pho-nay).

Available for $3.99 exclusively at Trader Joe's. 12.5% Alcohol.

2013 Grifone Sangiovese.

From the bottle:

This wine is inspired by the ancient history of our people and is a tribute to Juno, wife of Jupiter and Queen of the gods of ancient Rome, the protector of welfare of women overseeing all aspects of marriage, fertility, and childbirth. Sangiovese (literally Blood of Jupiter), Italy's most popular grape, is best suited to create a wine with complex character yet sufficiently delicate to appeal to those preferring smooth and fruit driven wines.

Notes of sweet fruits intertwine with hints of Mediterranean spices, vitalized by a bright acidity that is balanced by balsamic and fragrant flavors, extending its finish and inviting the next sip.

Sharing an intrinsic characteristic of all Italian wines, Sangiovese goes well with healthy foods made from quality ingredients. Try it chilled with light fare or with your favorite medley salad. The wine is especially suitable for pairing with vegetarian and vegan dishes.

The **2013 Grifone Sangiovese** begins with aromas of ripe cherry, strawberry, and raspberry along with a little anise and leather. This easy-to-drink wine tastes super ripe and perhaps slightly medicinal with lots of jammy sweet mixed berry and sour cherry fruit. A hint of an earthy undertone leads into the medium-length finish that features more lingering sweet fruit.

Taste Rating: 6   **Cost Rating: 10**

Overall Rating: 7.0

Recommended Buy

Second is 2012 La Granja Tempranillo from country Carinena, Aragon, Spain.

Available for $3.99 exclusively at Trader Joe's. 13% Alcohol.

From the bottle:
La Granja 360 (AKA the farm 360) winery is located in the North of Spain.

La Granja is there to entertain and bring happiness to all the people. A different wine—360° turnaround—for different people.

An everyday drinking soft rounded juicy red wine with ripe raspberry flavours.

A great match for barbeque roasted meat, grilled vegetables or cheeses.

2012 La Granja Tempranillo.

The **2012 La Granja Tempranillo** begins with aromas of black cherry, raspberry, a touch of cranberry, and cedar. This is a simple wine but it does benefit from some time to breathe. Black cherry, raspberry, strawberry, and a distinct earthy note are the primary flavors on this soft and easy wine. It ends dry with some unusual, but not unpleasant, lingering citrus notes.

Taste Rating: 6   **Cost Rating: 10**

Overall Rating: 7.0

Recommended Buy

Third, we have the 2012 Honey Moon Viognier from California.

Available for $5.99 exclusively at Trader Joe's. 13.5% Alcohol.

From the bottle:

2012 Honey Moon Viognier.

Viognier is a rare and stylish grape with golden hues and amazing floral scents. Our Honey Moon Viognier is named after the June Full Moon, which signifies the moment when the sweet scent of flowers turn into young grapes, creating this lush, full bodied wine with peach, apricot and honeysuckle aromas followed by luscious honey, mango and nectar finish.

Very perfumey, Viognier is beautiful with "exotic" recipes such as Thai coconut-based curries and many cheeses. It's also a tasty and unusual choice for dishes like simply prepared lobster, roast chicken, and plainly sauteed sole or trout.

The **2012 Honey Moon Viognier** begins with aromas of peach and citrus plus honeysuckle and other pleasant floral notes. The wine tastes sweet and simple with flavors of apricot, pears, peach, and a surprising note of banana that comes into play midpalate and lasts all the way into the finish. This medium-bodied wine is a bit flabby but it makes up for it with lots of pleasing flavors. There's even a hint of a mineral streak on the nice medium-length finish.

Taste Rating: 6 **Cost Rating: 10**

Overall Rating: 7.0

Recommended Buy

Last is the 2011 Epicuro Aglianico from Beneventano IGT, Campania, Italy.

Available for $5.99 exclusively at Trader Joe's. 13% Alcohol.

From the bottle:
> This red wine shows intense blackberry and cherry notes harmoniously exalted by a light spicy background. Smooth and velvety with a firm backbone. Perfect at 18° with red meat, ham, and mature cheeses.

2011 Epicuro Aglianico.

The **2011 Epicuro Aglianico** begins with aromas of blackberry and a little spice. The medium-bodied wine tastes smooth, soft, and simple with blackberry jam and cranberry fruit that's a bit on the syrupy side. Hints of smoked meat and anise are a nice surprise. It ends dry with good length.

Taste Rating: 6   Cost Rating: 10

Overall Rating: 7.0

Recommended Buy

MORE RECOMMENDED TRADER JOE'S EXCLUSIVE WINE:
- Albero Monastrell
- Caves Saint-Pierre Vacqueyras
- Conte di Bregonzo Amarone Della Valpolicella
- La Granja Syrah
- La Granja Tempranillo and Garnacha
- Spiral Wines Cabernet Sauvignon
- Trader Joe's Grand Reserve Lot 36 Petit Verdot
- Trader Joe's Reserve Paso Robles Syrah
- Tuella Douro

CHAPTER 8

BOX WINE

ONCE HIDDEN AWAY FROM JUDGING eyes behind coffee machines or stashed deep inside refrigerators, box wines have begun to come of age and can represent the ultimate value for wine drinkers. The only problem is winnowing the wheat from the chaff because there's still a whole lot of boxed plonk out there. I have tasted every imaginable box wine I could find, ranging in price from $10 to $50+, to bring you the very best of the bunch. But first, why box wine?

- **Convenience**—The typical box is three liters (3L), which is the equivalent of four bottles. Boxes are easy to buy, easy to transport from the store (seriously, try carrying eight bottles of wine in your arms and then compare that to just two boxes), and easy to use—no corkscrew necessary and always ready, whether you just want a smidge or you need to (discreetly) fill your Starbucks Trenta cup. Boating, picnics, and camping are all much easier with a box.
- **Cost**—Not only do you save on boxed wine because you're buying in bulk but also because the packaging costs a fraction of traditional glass bottlings for the same amount of wine. Since the 3L box packaging weighs about the same as a single glass bottle, there are also massive savings in shipping costs, which in theory get passed on to you.
- **Freshness**—Boxed wine stays fresh for four to six weeks once opened. Even the best preservation methods for a bottle of wine will only save it for a few days, but with the vacu-

um-sealed pouches used today box wine stays as good as new for weeks after you pour the first glass.

- **No Cork Taint**—And last but not least, box wine puts an end to worries about cork taint, which affects a surprising number of bottles. Cork taint comes from TCA, a chemical substance that can be present in corks that kills the flavors normally present in wines and replaces them with moldy or musty aromas. You've likely encountered a bottle affected with cork taint yourself and just assumed it was a wine you didn't like and therefore did not purchase again.

In tasting all these boxes, they seemed to divide generally into two camps: those that focus on keeping the wine as cheap as possible while still producing something drinkable versus those that are focused much more on the quality of the wine but package their wine, in boxes for convenience or for environmental reasons. (The carbon footprint for box wine is less than half that of the equivalent bottles.) As you might guess the quality of wine is significantly better in the second group.

It's also interesting to note that while the trend in bottled wines has been to higher alcohol reds (14–16 percent alcohol), very few of these boxes cross the 13 percent alcohol level. My guess is that this is simply another cost-saving measure, as the excise tax for wine increases once alcohol level hits 14 percent. This does raise some concerns, as it could mean producers are putting too much focus on their costs rather than on quality— that is, are they sacrificing the quality of the wine to keep the alcohol percentage artificially low? I have my suspicions, although no definitive answers, but it's certainly something to watch for in this growing segment.

Vinchio-Vaglio Serra Piemonte Barbera 2012—
A True Bulk Buy

100% Barbera from Piedmont, Italy. 12.5% Alcohol.

Suggested Retail Price: $24. Available for as low as $16 for the 3L box.

From the importer:
> This wine is an entry level Barbera from Vinchio Vaglio Serra, a winery known for their excellent Barbera production. Their winemaker, Giuliano Noe, has brought about a Barbera revival with his excellent wines, and even the entry level Barbera from VVS was not left out. Barbera is a wine that is easy to pair with many meals. Antipasti of meats, cheese, and olives, poultry and red meat are all great compliments to the Piemonte Barbera. Fresh, red fruit and a pleasing palate make this wine an easy choice for all occasions.

Box wine from Piedmont? Yes, even the land of Barolo makes a box wine and it's fabulous.

The **2012 Vinchio-Vaglio Serra Piemonte Barbera** begins with an aroma filled with abundant amounts of black cherry. There are hints of plum, spice, and even a little mint, but it's the wonderful black cherry that will have your nose returning to the glass over and over. Tasting the wine reveals more black cherry (no surprise), plum, and just a whole lot of juicy dark fruit. A little spice kicks in midpalate and lasts all the way through the long finish. The whole thing is wrapped up in a smooth and silky texture. Truth be told, it comes off as a bit one dimensional at first sip, but magic happens when you pair it with food. Pasta in red sauce, pizza, beef stew—it's fantastic with them all. The best part is that we purchased it for just $16, which is the equivalent of a $4 bottle. A Bulk Buy in the truest sense of the term!

Taste Rating: 8   Cost Rating: 10
Overall Rating: 8.5
Bulk Buy

Big House White 2013—*A Kitchen Sink Blend*

A blend of Gruner Veltliner, Gewurztraminer, Viognier, Malvasia Bianca, Sauvignon Blanc, and other white varieties from California. 13.5% Alcohol.

Suggested Retail Price: $20. Available widely for around $17.

From the box:

> Yadda, yadda, yadda, Warden! Break outta the confines of stuffy tradition with this no tool required tradition. Cagney or Robinson would never deem it a dirty box. Big House White is an unpretentious blend from a handful of nonconformist grape varieties. We start with vibrant varietals to make the skeleton, add a fruit-forward blend for a structured mid-palate and top it off with something aromatic. This floral, tropical White more than sing-sings for its supper. Best enjoyed chilled.

This wine definitely meets the requirements to be called a kitchen sink blend—the informal name given to nontraditional blends of many different grapes.

The **2013 Big House White** is a sure conversation starter. With its engaging packaging and mongrel-like makeup of under-the-radar varietals there's plenty of intrigue even before you crack it open. Don't let the whimsical packaging lure you into thinking that there isn't a serious wine inside, however. The wine opens with a very pleasant, very aromatic nose of peach, pear, a little banana, tropical fruit, and floral notes. If flavorful wines are your thing, this one also delivers when tasting with tart tropical fruit, zesty citrus, peach, pear, and the continuation of those hints of banana from the nose. Refreshing and easy to drink but not in that California watered-down Pinot Grigio way, it ends crisp and long with lingering tart citrus and tropical fruit.

Taste Rating: 7   **Cost Rating: 10**
Overall Rating: 7.8
Highly Recommended

Alain Jaume & Fils Grand Veneur Côtes du Rhône Reserve 2012—*A Dynamite Daily Drinker*

A blend of 60% Grenache and 40% Syrah from Côtes du Rhône, France. 14% Alcohol.

Suggested Retail Price: $43. Available for as low as $35.

From the box:

Since 1826, from father to son, we have been following a philosophy with simple principles: "A great wine is made with perfect quality grapes yielding an expression of the earth."

The "Reserve Grand Veneur" red is elaborated according to respect of the Tradition, using the typical Rhone Valley grape varieties: 60 percent Grenache, 40 percent Syrah.

Elegant and well balanced, this wine will seduce you with its red fresh fruit aromas (cherry, strawberry, raspberry) and its spicy hint of black pepper and liquorice. Ideally served at 60F, this wine will make a perfect combination if served with Mediterranean cuisine, grilled red meats or cheese.

This is a wine that you can also buy in a traditional 750ml bottle. Two things stand out about this:

- Savings. Bottles of this wine sells for around $15 apiece. Since the 3L box holds the equivalent of four bottles, you're effectively paying around $35 for what would otherwise cost closer to $60.
- Quality. We have often found that if a box wine is also sold in a bottle, it's generally a sign of good quality. (It's not a fail-safe indicator but there does seem to be a trend.)

The **2012 Alain Jaume & Fils Grand Veneur Côtes du Rhône Reserve** presents with a lovely nose that gets even better with air. Aromas of smoked meat and leather when first poured give way to black cherry and wild berry fruit flavors in short order. Nice touches of spice and lavender are present as well. Tasting this smooth and silky blend reveals classic Côtes du Rhône and offers a combination of taste and complexity that I would be more than happy to drink every day. It ends dry and grippy with more dark fruit and even a bit of graphite minerality.

Taste Rating: 8   **Cost Rating: 8**

Overall Rating: 8.0

Highly Recommended

Black Box Platinum Central Coast Cabernet Sauvignon 2012—*The Evolution of the Black Box*

78% Cabernet Sauvignon, 10% Syrah, 5% Petite Sirah, 3% Malbec, 1% Cabernet Franc, 1% Merlot, and 2% other red varieties from Central Coast, California. 13.6% Alcohol.

Suggested Retail Price: $30. Available for as low as $26.

From the box:

Black Box Platinum symbolizes our devotion to crafting high-quality wines of superior value. We source from only the finest growing regions to create intense fruit flavors, exceptional texture and unparalleled elegance.

Smooth and enticing with ripe cherry, blackberry and toasty oak flavors and a lengthy finish. This wine comes from the Central Coast, a premier appellation known for its perfect blend of cooling fog, wind and warm sun.

One of the original mass market boxes, the evolution of the Black Box is a fascinating look at the economics behind boxed wines. When the Black Box Cabernet was first introduced it was sourced from Paso Robles, California. As demand grew that sourcing was changed to all of California. Then just a few years ago that sourcing was changed again, but this time to the Central Valley of Chile. None of this is necessarily bad (Chile makes some really excellent Cabernet Sauvignon) but it demonstrates an issue that all box wines must face—how do you maintain quality and supply in a growing market while still maintaining your price point? Vintages vary every year, sometimes drastically, but demand does not.

One solution to this is to do exactly what Black Box did and try to maintain a high level of quality by changing the sourcing of their grapes. Another solution would be to raise prices. As it turns out, Black Box has, in a way, now done both. Those wistfully longing for the days California Cabernet in their Black Box will be happy to see the new Platinum Series of wines from the Central Coast of California. Priced at $5 more than the normal Black Box (SRP of $29.99 versus $24.99) the wines are available in Colorado and Minnesota initially with a nationwide rollout in the near future. Let's take a look at how the Cabernet tastes, shall we?

The **2012 Black Box Platinum Central Coast Cabernet Sauvignon** begins with very pleasant aromas of plum, black cherry, some lovely spice, a hint of mint, and a bit of cigar box. Tasting reveals sweet, rich, and ripe blackberry with nice touches of spice and cola. You'll also find a nice smooth texture and a bit of toasty oak, but this wine is driven by the rich dark berry fruit. Normally I prefer completely dry wines and, like a lot of reds in boxes, this one is slightly sweet (6.2g/L of residual sugar) but it really works. It ends long with lots of lingering blackberry and touches of vanilla. This is really quite yummy stuff!

The only question that remains is whether they can maintain the quality of the wine as they increase the supply for a national roll-out. For that we'll have to wait and see, but in the meantime if you can get your hands on the 2012 vintage I recommend it, especially at the equivalent of about $6.50 per bottle!

Taste Rating: 7   **Cost Rating: 9**

Overall Rating: 7.5

Recommended Buy

Esporao Alandra White 2013—*A Light and Highly Quaffable Wine*

A blend of Antao Vaz, Perrum, and Arinto from Alentejo, Portugal. 12.5% Alcohol.

Suggested Retail Price: $26. Available for around $20.

From the box:

> We have combined the best selection of unique local grapes to produce this wine. Blended and bottled by Esporao. The diversity of its origin determines the freshness, balance and versatility of this wine.
>
> The Alandra wines result from the diversity and uniqueness of Portugal's grape varieties and our winemaker's creative and contemporary approach. We made this wine for daily meals, to be shared along with creamy cheeses, tuna salad, grilled fish, or tempura.

We've talked a lot about the extreme value coming out of Portugal, so it seems like a natural spot to look for box wine. Unfortunately, you won't find much available here in the United States, but pay attention when you do.

This wine is a perfect example. Coming from seventeen-year-old vines grown in granite/schist rock with clay/loam soil, it's a blend of three grapes you won't see much of outside of Spain and Portugal. It's also a dry wine, which means that the other qualities inherent in the grape really need to shine through since they won't be covered up by a whole bunch of sweet sugar.

The **2013 Esporao Alandra Branco (White)** begins with a fruity aroma filled with pear, apple, orange, a little apricot, nice floral notes, and a bit of spice. This light-bodied wine tastes simple, fresh, and quite good with lots of apple, some zesty citrus, and a bit of mango and pineapple. That little streak of spice from the nose carries over as well and there are even touches of sea salt that lead into the dry, medium-long finish. This is a fresh, light, and highly quaffable wine that you'll be quite glad comes in a box.

Taste Rating: 7   **Cost Rating: 10**
Overall Rating: 7.8
Highly Recommended

Vina Borgia Garnacha 2013—*A Beauty of a Box from Bodegas Borsao*

100% Garnacha from Campo de Borja, Aragon, Spain. 14% Alcohol.

Suggested Retail Price: $25. Available for around $20. Bottles sell for around $6–$7, so this 3L box (four-bottle equivalent) at only $20 is a great deal on an already inexpensive wine.

From the box:

> From the heart of Aragon, birthplace of Garnacha, comes Vina Borgia. The wine is a perfect example of the varietal characteristics: dark cherries and blueberries mingle on the palate and are accented by light peppery notes. Fresh bright flavors are balanced by a fine structure and long finish. The wine is meticulously crafted for your immediate enjoyment.

Bodegas Borsao, the maker of this wine, is one of our very favorite producers of one of our very favorite value varieties—Spanish Garnacha. In fact, I don't believe we've reviewed a Bodegas Borsao wine that we didn't rate a Bulk Buy. Why should that change when the wine is packaged in a box instead of a bottle?

The **2013 Vina Borgia Garnacha** begins with a pleasant aroma of blackberry, blueberry, raspberry, black cherry, licorice, and a bit of spice. The wine tastes delicious with tons of juicy dark berry fruit and streaks of peppery spice. The licorice notes from the nose also continue in this smooth, almost creamy wine with good acidity. A bit of an earthy streak leads into the dry finish that features lingering tart plum and other dark berry fruit. Wonderful.

Taste Rating: 8   **Cost Rating: 10**

Overall Rating: 8.5

Bulk Buy

The Original House Wine Riesling—*Everything You Want in a Box Wine, Despite What You Might Suspect from the Label*

Riesling from the Pacific Northwest. 11% Alcohol.

Suggested Retail Price: $22. Available for as low as $14.

From the box:

My House is Your House.
A beautiful aromatic nose filled with pineapple, honeysuckle and peach notes. The juicy palate marries pear and clover honey with ripe banana on the crisp finish.

While it's hard to draw any conclusions about a wine from its label, there are a few things that raise questions for us. One is a non-vintage status. Not necessarily bad in and of itself, it can mean (especially in inexpensive wine) that the sourcing of the wine can vary quite a bit year to year. Basically the winery is giving itself the leeway to blend wine from different vintages together if necessary. Like I said, this is not necessarily a bad thing, but it does make it awfully hard to judge if the wine you tasted a year ago is going to taste anything like the wine you buy today because you have no idea if it is from the same supply (like you would if it were labeled with a vintage).

Another rule of thumb we follow when buying wine we haven't tried before is to look for wines that list a specific region, and the smaller the better. The larger the region, the more wines that were likely blended together—again not necessarily a bad thing but it makes it hard to know what you are getting year to year. Based on these two things we were a little worried about the **Original House Wine Riesling** before tasting it based on the non-vintage status and the extremely large "American Wine" region on the box, but have no fear this is quite a good wine.

A nose with light aromas of pear, honeysuckle, and a little pineapple turns into a very flavorful and refreshing wine when tasting. Not too sweet and not too dry, this box has a lot of great Riesling character. Juicy pear, apple, some lemon/lime, and a bit of tropical fruit are lightly soaked in honey and a touch of nutmeg. On the finish the juicy fruit turns tart and leaves you with lingering pineapple and continuing nutmeg notes. Refreshing and really easy to drink with lots of flavor, this has everything you want in a box wine despite what you might suspect by looking at the label.

Taste Rating: 7   **Cost Rating: 10**
Overall Rating: 7.8
Highly Recommended

Esporao Alandra Red 2013—*Another Dynamite Daily Drinker*

A blend of Moreto, Castelao, and Trincadeira from Alentejo, Portugal. 13% Alcohol.

Suggested Retail Price: $26. Available for around $20.

From the winemaker:
> Entry point wine with a fresh and fruity profile, obtained from blending a wide range of wines to guarantee a consistent quality.
>
> Harvest Year: Excellent year for red wines in this region. The low winter rainfall contributed to a smaller than average grape harvest with deeply concentrated high quality wines.
> Soil Type: Granite/schist rock with clay/loam soil.
> Average age of vines: 10 years.

Just like the Esporao Alandra White, this box is made up of a blend of varieties you've likely never heard of before, but don't let that give you pause—this is one tasty wine. The **2013 Esporao Alandra Tinto** (Red) opens with a pleasant and fruity aroma of black cherry, blueberry, raspberry, and just a hint of anise. In the mouth you'll find lots of smooth and juicy fruit with touches of spice and leather. This medium- to full-bodied wine has good acidity and a surprisingly long and grippy finish. Quite good, this wine makes for a great daily drinker.

Taste Rating: 7   Cost Rating: 10

Overall Rating: 7.8

Highly Recommended

La Petite Frog Picpoul De Pinet 2013—*The Little Frog in the Big Box That Will Have You Jumping for Joy*

100% Picpoul from Languedoc, Languedoc-Roussillon, France. 12.5% Alcohol.

Suggested Retail Price: $34. Available for as low as $24.

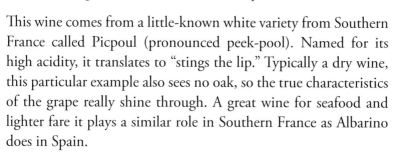

From the bottle:
Crisp and fruit drive, this dry white wine goes well with fish, chicken or pasta dishes.

This wine comes from a little-known white variety from Southern France called Picpoul (pronounced peek-pool). Named for its high acidity, it translates to "stings the lip." Typically a dry wine, this particular example also sees no oak, so the true characteristics of the grape really shine through. A great wine for seafood and lighter fare it plays a similar role in Southern France as Albarino does in Spain.

The **2013 La Petite Frog Picpoul De Pinet** begins with very pleasant aromas of green apple, pear, lemon, lime, a little nectarine, and honeysuckle. Tasting the wine reveals it is true to its name with great acidity. The wine is light- to medium-bodied but full of flavor with deep, rich, tart fruit like zesty citrus, peach, and more nectarine and lemon/lime notes. It ends crisply with a dry mouthwatering finish. At only $24 for a box (the equivalent of $6 a bottle), this little frog will have you jumping for joy!

Taste Rating: 8   Cost Rating: 10

Overall Rating: 8.5

Bulk Buy

MORE RECOMMENDED BOX WINE:
- Duca Del Frassino Garganega/Pinot Grigio
- Fuori Strada Off Road Sangiovese
- Jack Tone Vineyards White Blend
- La Vieille Ferme Rouge
- Lieb Cellars Bridge Lane White Blend
- Maison Cubi Carignan Syrah
- Pepperwood Grove The Big Green Box Pinot Noir
- Target Cube Sauvignon Blanc
- Wineberry Domaine de Garrigon Côtes du Rhône

APPENDIX 1

RESOURCES

The Website: www.ReverseWineSnob.com

There are links to all our Costco and Trader Joe's reviews right in the header, along with our latest Top 10 lists, the Wine Ranking Database, and the Wine Deals page we referenced multiple times in the book.

While you are there also be sure to sign up for our daily emails to never miss a recommended wine and receive notifications of special sales and promotions from partners just for readers of *The Reverse Wine Snob.*

You can also follow us on social media for more great content!

Facebook: http://facebook.com/ReverseWineSnob

Twitter: @ReverseWineSnob: http://twitter.com/ReverseWineSnob

Pinterest: http://pinterest.com/reversewinesnob/

Google+: https://plus.google.com/+ReverseWineSnob

Instagram: http://instagram.com/reversewinesnob

APPENDIX 2

WINE RANKING DATABASE

Here's some information on how to best use the Wine Ranking Database at ReverseWineSnob.com.

The Wine Ranking database contains all of the wines I've reviewed along with their score and links to the reviews themselves. Clicking on the names of any of the columns will allow you to sort and filter. So for example, say you want a list of my top-rated Malbecs. Simply hover over "Variety," click on the red menu button that appears, and filter based on Malbec.

You can then sort the resulting dataset by any of the columns to further refine your results. A few other important features to note: to search within the database, click the magnifying glass at the top left.

On the top right, under the red "Menu" button, you'll find the option to share and next to it the option to view the dataset full-screen.

This is an important option to note! Once you go into full-screen mode you'll be able to save any views that you create for future reference. So if you created a list of the highest-rated Malbecs, you can save it and then come back at any time and see an up-to-date list.

To see the customized views you've created, download, discuss, embed, or print simply click on the red "Menu" button at the top right. Clicking on "More Views" will allow you to see not only your own saved views but also a number that I and others have created. So go give it a try! I typically add the newest reviews to the database once or twice a month. All of this is run through the excellent Socrata Social Data Player.

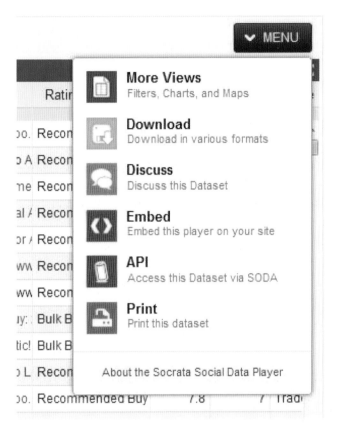